$S\pi$

HOW TO SERVE GOD
IN A MARXIST LAND

HOW TO SERVE GOD

IN A MARXIST LAND

by KARL BARTH

and JOHANNES HAMEL

with an introductory essay

by ROBERT McAFEE BROWN

ASSOCIATION PRESS • NEW YORK

CONTENTS

1102303

PUBLISHER'S NOTE

Many people have been involved in providing this book of materials for Americans. The authorized translation into English of Karl Barth's *Letter to a Pastor in the German Democratic Republic* was made by Henry Clark and James D. Smart, of Union Theological Seminary, New York. This letter was originally published by Evangelischer Verlag Zollikon in 1958, under the title *Brief an einen Pfarrer in der DDR*. It is translated and published fully in the United States now for the first time, with their permission and on authorization of Karl Barth.

Thomas Wieser, of the United Student Christian Council, made the authorized translation into English of *An Answer to Karl Barth from East Germany*, by Johannes Hamel. This was first printed as "Antwort an Karl Barth" in *Kirchenblatt für die Reformierte Schweiz*, March, 1959.

Mr. Wieser also made the authorized translation into English of the essay by Johannes Hamel, "The Proclamation of the Gospel in the Marxist World," which originally appeared as his contribution to *Gottesdienst—Menschendienst, Festschrift für Eduard*

Thurneysen, published by Evangelischer Verlag Zollikon, 1958.

All material is used by permission. Without the initiative and assistance of Mrs. Marguerite Wieser, these writings would not have been brought together in this book.

HOW TO SERVE GOD
IN A MARXIST LAND

INTRODUCTORY ESSAY

by Robert McAfee Brown

This is one "how-to" book that isn't offering Easy Rules for Success. In fact, if there is one over-all theme in the pages that follow, it is that in trying to serve God in a Marxist land, Rule Number One goes: There are no Easy Rules for Success. This doesn't mean that discussion of the problem therefore ceases, but that discussion of the problem therefore becomes more important than ever before. Christians faced with perplexing issues must always try to "talk them out" together, believing that if the interchange is conducted in the light of Scripture, God can use the interchange to help His children discern His will more clearly.

"How to serve God in a Marxist land" is obviously a burning issue for any Christian living behind the Iron Curtain. And it ought to concern Christians living in the West as well, for at least two reasons. First of all, we need to become sympathetically aware of what is happening to our Christian brethren in other parts of the world: "If one member suffers, all suffer together" (1 Corinthians 12:26). Secondly, we need to realize that we have much to learn from fellow Christians who are facing ethical dilemmas that at least on the surface seem much more agonizing and difficult and acute than ours. It may be salutary for us to discover that—as these writings show—the agonizing, difficult, acute dilemmas are not all concentrated on one side of the Iron Curtain.

The incident that refocused the problem in the minds of Americans was a typically sensationalistic newspaper account, several months ago, of a letter Karl Barth had written to an East German pastor, on the problem of serving God in a Marxist land. The dispatch reported only a few rather extreme statements from the letter, which, taken out of context, put Barth in the worst possible light and suggested that he was practically a Communist informer. There was a great deal of subsequent comment on Barth's letter in the American press, most of it based on a few brief extracts from the letter, which actually ran to forty-five pages in the German edition. In the present volume, this letter is translated into English *in full* for the first time. Thus it is only from this text that a significant appraisal and critique can be made. Karl Barth has never been one to inspire lukewarm reactions, and part of the value of an "occasional" piece, such as the present letter, is that it can and does invite vigorous rejoinders.

In his letter, Barth refers to an essay by Johannes

Hamel which had been published only a few months earlier in a *Festschrift* for Eduard Thurneysen, a life-long friend of Barth's, entitled "The Proclamation of the Gospel in the Marxist World." No portions of this essay have previously appeared in English, and its publication in the present volume is a notable addition to the materials available on the problem of the life of the church in a world dominated by the Marxist gospel. Pastor Hamel knows whereof he speaks. He has been proclaiming the gospel in the Marxist world for well over a decade. For ten years he was pastor to students at the University of Halle, where he often had Bible classes of over 1,000 students. He has paid the price of arrest and imprisonment for his convictions, so that without trying to glamorize his story it can be said very directly that his courage has earned him the right to be heard. He is likewise the author of the brief answer to Barth's letter included in this volume, which indicates the kind of reception that Barth's comments received in East Germany, where what he had to say was both warmly praised and roundly condemned.

I

In order to see the famous Barth letter in the clearest possible context, it will be wise to consider first of all the less well-known but equally important essay by Hamel, since it is written out of precisely the kind of situation to which Barth is attempting to speak.

Pastor Hamel is like many other men who, at the end of World War II, found themselves living in a sector of Germany which, largely as a result of a geographical accident of war, was under the control of Russian Communists. The Christian pastors were faced with the very perplexing problem of discovering how the gospel could be proclaimed under a regime which was actively hostile to that gospel. Many Americans, bred on the most vigorous kind of anti-Communist propaganda, tend to feel that the gospel *cannot* be proclaimed in a Marxist world, and that anybody who stays and tries to do so must by that very act have sold out to the regime in power. They feel that the really prophetic Christian must either be captured or escape to the West where religion is respected and honored. But it is not necessarily a prophetic thing to be preaching in the safety of lands where "religion is respected and honored," and it is not necessarily a prophetic action to leave the difficult situation where God has placed one in order to avoid the dilemmas— and dangers—which may result. And there are Christian pastors like Johannes Hamel who have not tried to escape, but who have stayed behind the Iron Curtain in order that they may engage in the infinitely perplexing task of seeking day by day to relate their Christian faith with directness and courage to a very un-Christian situation.

Some day the story of these men will be told, and it will be an epic chapter in the history of the church of Christ under persecution. At the present time, those of us in the West do not know very much about how they have been able to serve God in a Marxist land. And we must first of all recognize that we are not morally entitled to the easy posture of condemning them for what we may too easily assume to have been "capitulation to the demands of a totalitarian state." We need above all to listen to what they say about what they are trying to do; and the essay by Johannes Hamel gives us the chance to do just that.

Since this is a fairly long and complex essay, it will be helpful first of all to give a brief summary of its main points. The author begins by urging us to avoid stereotypes of the Marxist world. We must not be betrayed into interpreting Marxism by its own presuppositions, nor by any presuppositions other than those which biblical faith provides for us. As Christians, he says, we must realize that the phenomenon of Marxism exists in a world in which "the principalities and powers" have already been overcome by Jesus Christ. This world is God's world; and Marxism must therefore be understood as something which exists within God's world, and which cannot ultimately and finally threaten God's sovereignty.

This is followed by descriptions of four situations from biblical history, in which the people of God found themselves under the oppressive rule of alien and pagan powers. The four situations described are the overlordship of Assyria in the eighth century B.C.; of Babylon in the seventh and sixth centuries B.C.; the domination of Persia in the sixth century B.C.; and the subjugation of the early Christians under Roman rule in the first century A.D.

The question must now be faced: In what ways does the Bible give us direction when we too have to live under a regime which does not acknowledge the reality of the God we worship? The next section of the essay points out some of the lessons which can be drawn from the biblical examples cited above. Pastor Hamel finds that there is a significant alternative both to revolt (i.e., open opposition) and to alignment (i.e., submission). It is the alternative suggested by such passages of Scripture as Isaiah 10, where the pagan power, Assyria, is understood as "the rod of God's anger," and "the staff of God's fury." The same theme is traced in various portions of the New Testament, particularly in Paul (Romans 13), and in 1 Peter, an epistle written during a time of persecution. This appraisal of the role of the dominant power rules out either revolt or alignment, and makes it necessary for the church to walk a precarious kind of path, but a path which presents real opportunities for the church and its proclamation of the gospel.

Pastor Hamel highlights four facets of this approach: (1) the foreign powers and their rulers must be seen as "God's instruments," i.e., means which he can employ in the carrying out of his purposes; (2) they must be seen as agents of God's judgment, and the message which the Christian hears in their activity must therefore be a call to repentance; (3) it must be recognized that the promise of redemption is always present in the midst of judgment, and that out of what appears to be grievous evil, God can nevertheless work good; and finally (4) the Christian may never forget that God remains the Lord of history, and that God is God even in the midst of Babylon. This being so, the Christian may find himself called upon to live out his Christian witness right in the midst of Babylon.

After this analysis of the biblical materials relevant to his subject, Hamel devotes the remainder of the essay to an attempt to apply these biblical insights to the central problem of "the proclamation of the gospel in the Marxist world." There are a number of points in this section that are worth highlighting for our purposes. For one thing, the author counsels us at considerable length to avoid attacking *or* defending the Marxist order for what can only be called crude anti-Communist or pro-Communist reasons. He gives telling examples of the mentality of each position.

What, then, is the real issue? The real issue is whether or not the Christian Church in the Marxist world can really believe that *God* is meeting her in these encounters with Marxism—and Marxists. Hamel makes the very bold statement that the Marxists can be seen as "servants of God," even though they do not, of course, acknowledge that they are such, and would either vehemently or amusedly deny such a description of themselves. And since these words will surely

sound offensive and even shocking to Western ears,
it should be pointed out that Hamel is speaking
here in nothing other than the terms that Isaiah 10
uses to describe the despotic Assyrians. He is trying
to say that in God's world God can use even the
Marxist for the fulfilling of his own purposes, even
though, like the Assyrian, the Marxist "does not so
intend, and his mind does not so think" (Isaiah 10:7).

There is another issue that the Christian must face
as he wrestles with the problem of proclaiming the
gospel in a Marxist land. Is the Christian willing to
hear the Marxist critique of the church without either
accepting it in terms of Marxist presuppositions, or
becoming so defensive in the face of it that he turns
to uncritical defense of the existing activities of the
church? Here Hamel is obviously describing actual
reactions by Christians to what Marxists have said
about the church. It becomes a betrayal of the gospel
simply to accept the Marxist criticisms of Christianity,
and particularly "organized Christianity," from the
standpoint of Marxist ideology. But it is no less a
betrayal of the gospel for Christians to close ranks
and refuse to listen to the critique simply because it
is being made by nonbelievers.

This suggests, therefore, an important further in-
gredient in the situation. This is the absolute necessity of *repentance* in the life of the church. Behind
all of the human accusations about the inadequacy,
the impotence, and the irrelevance of the church,
the Christian must listen for the voice of God. God's

accusation must be heard for what it is, and his saving act must be recognized in the very midst of this human judgment. It is Hamel's contention that an attitude of this sort can free the Christian from the necessity of being a fellow traveler of Marxism or a fellow traveler of anti-Marxism.

In these terms it is possible to see why Hamel can describe so enthusiastically the vivid and immediate relevance which the Bible has for Christians living behind the Iron Curtain today.

The essay concludes with a call to Christians to recognize that in different kinds of political situations, they will understand their political responsibilities in different ways. He urges Christians outside the Marxist orbit to make a real effort to understand that Christians inside the Marxist orbit must address the gospel *to Marxists,* unless they are going to be irrelevant in the situation where God has placed them.

II

How are Western, non-Marxist, "capitalist" Americans to appraise this essay? It is safe to assume that to many English-speaking readers the viewpoint Hamel expresses will be almost totally new, either in its theological perspective or its practical conclusions, or both. It is therefore all the more important that it be read seriously and carefully, with the realization that English-speaking readers may have some important things to learn from it.

Perhaps the most important thing to see at work
here is Hamel's genuine wrestling with a contemporary problem in the light of biblical faith. He does
not just pluck a verse from here and there, but tries
to examine his own situation in the light of the *full*
sweep of the history of the people of God. His starting
point is not Marxist ideology. It is not Western
democratic ideology. His starting point is the Bible.

As he looks at the world through biblical eyes,
Hamel realizes that this world, even this difficult
world of East Germany, is the world which is under
the sovereign sway of the living God. It is the world
into which the very Son of God entered, in which he
did battle with "the principalities and powers," and
in which he conquered them. *He* is the Lord of this
world, not someone in Moscow or Washington. Everything one sees in this world must be seen from the
perspective of this faith. This means that the Christian cannot abdicate from the task of trying to live
responsibly wherever God has placed him. And it
means seeing the given situation where God has
placed that Christian as a situation in which and
through which God is *saying* something and *doing*
something, using (with a kind of divine nonchalance)
whatever means come to hand, whether they be the
Assyrian empire or the Persian empire, the Roman
overlords or the Marxist overlords. So the Christian
must endeavor to see God at work in and through
the given events of world history.

All of this, it seems to me, is incontestably biblical;

and Hamel, rather than being accused of having said something "new" and original, should rather be described as having tried to take the New Testament seriously, and then having looked at the whole history of the people of God, in Old and New Testaments, in the light of it. Isaiah 10 is a key passage which the reader should re-examine if he wishes to see what Hamel is saying in biblical terms—but Isaiah 10 as read in the light of Paul's assertion in Colossians concerning the cosmic victory of Jesus Christ.

Does this mean, then, that the adoption of the biblical-theological perspective, so rapidly sketched above, leads with a kind of inevitability to the specific conclusions to which Hamel comes vis-à-vis the present Communist government in East Germany? Here we need to see Hamel in his own context, and not try to put him in our context. It would not necessarily follow that if he were a pastor in East Lansing or Amarillo or Spokane, he would be led by his biblical faith to the specific political conclusions expressed in his essay; for, as he points out, "The task of Christians to recognize and accept political responsibility in accordance with their faith and their ethics is commensurate to the opportunities which are actually open to them in any given situation." But by the same token it follows that a Christian in East Lansing or Amarillo or Spokane should not be too hasty in concluding that Hamel is not sufficiently critical of the government under which he lives— particularly in the light of the fact that the Commu-

nists have found it impossible to make Hamel play
their game on their terms. The American reader
needs to take with utter seriousness the way in which
Hamel refuses to speak from Marxist presuppositions,
and tries instead to speak from Christian presuppositions to that segment of the world which has, temporarily at least, accepted Marxist presuppositions.

The perplexing dilemma which Hamel's essay highlights is how to know when, from the biblical
orientation described above, the power of the state
has become so demonic that it can no longer be
viewed as an instrumentality of God, but must rather
be seen as an instrumentality of evil working against
God, which must therefore be opposed, in the name
of God and the gospel. It is clear that Hamel does
not view Marxism in this way, though it is clear that
both he and Barth did so view Nazism. (One cannot
imagine Hamel or Barth saying about the Nazi state
the same things that they say about the Communist
state.) And as to whether Hamel's assessment of the
Marxist as the "servant of God" is in any sense
descriptive, or must be rejected as a failure to measure
accurately enough the demonic power of Marxism—
this is a decision which every Christian must make
within the depths of his own soul. That most Christians in the West unhesitatingly make the latter
assessment is all the more reason for them to read
Hamel's essay with as much openness as possible.

There are, of course, other points along the way
where the reader will wish that he could press Hamel

further. *Is* the church, for example, freed from the responsibility of developing "theories about the nature of the state," as Hamel suggests toward the end of his essay? *Is* our place "below the powers and the rulers"? Does not all this smack a little too much of the Lutheran doctrine of the "two realms," which in the past has so often led to an attitude of acquiescence on the part of Christians toward rank injustice in the activities of the state? In lesser lives than Hamel's, this can be the beginning of an approach which ends by sanctifying the *status quo,* whatever *status quo* it may be. At the very least, a caution flag should be hoisted at this point.

There is another difficulty which arises when one sees God's activity in history too precisely. Is the pattern of God's historical working quite as coherent as Hamel, and many others, seem to think? Can we be as sure as we might like to be that these *specific* events are the ways in which God is positively working out his purposes, when these events may be ones in which God's purposes will be at least temporarily thwarted if his children do not rise up in protest?

This problem is closely related to a final problem—again a variant of the others—which can be stated by asking, "Where and how does the Christian finally draw the line between capitulation to a government (which may actually be an evil government) and revolt against a government (which may actually be a relatively good government)?" Hamel, as we have seen, denies that these need to be the alternatives, at

least in East Germany today. At the very least, he has
sketched a compelling statement of another possible
alternative. It is even possible that he has done much
more, and laid the groundwork for a recovery of a
"biblical politics," albeit a precarious politics, subject
to the kinds of difficulties stated above.

III

Some of these basic and deep-seated questions can be
brought into sharper focus by turning to look at
Karl Barth's *Letter to a Pastor in the German Democratic Republic*. Our examination of the Hamel essay
gives us a context into which we may fit Barth's letter,
but before we look at the letter itself we must engage
in the further task of fitting the letter into the context
of the development of Barth's own thought.

Swiss by birth, Barth was a professor at the University of Bonn in Germany when Hitler came to power
in 1932. He very soon became aware of the danger
and menace of Nazism, and from 1933 on was increasingly outspoken in his condemnation of it. He lost
his University post almost immediately because he
refused to take the required oath of allegiance to
Hitler. During the years up to 1939 he turned out
an astonishing number of essays, articles, and pamphlets, warning his fellow Christians of the demonic
character of Nazism, and particularly of the subtle
ways in which it was making inroads into the life of
the church. He was incensed by the activity of the

so-called "German Christians," who engaged in an almost total embrace of Adolf Hitler and welcomed him as a new messiah sent to the church and the German nation.

Barth was active in the formulation of the Barmen Declaration of 1934, which began with a stirring and unequivocal affirmation of the sole lordship of Jesus Christ, thereby making plain that no other "lords" could claim any place in the life of the church. The first article was as follows:

> Jesus Christ, as He is attested to us in Holy Scripture, is the one Word of God, whom we have to hear and whom we have to trust and obey in life and in death. We condemn the false doctrine that the Church can and must recognize as God's revelation other events and powers, forms and truths apart from and alongside this one Word of God.

That this is still Barth's position is symbolized by the fact that he quotes the first paragraph above at the very beginning of the latest volume of his *Church Dogmatics*[1] as normative for his approach to ethics in that volume.

In such pamphlets as *Theological Existence Today, Church and State,* and *The Church and the Political Question Today,* Barth made his position of active opposition to Nazism clearer and clearer. In the latter pamphlet, for example, he asserts that the church cannot remain indifferent to Nazism, or adopt a pose

1 Cf. Barth, *Die Kirchliche Dogmatik,* IV, 3 (Erste Hälfte), p. 1.

of neutrality when confronted by it. Nazism is not only a political movement, it is a religious movement. Furthermore, it represents the dissolution of the just state, and the church must have a concern that the state be just. Opposition to Nazism is a political decision, but it is prescribed by the decision of faith. The church must pray for the destruction of Nazism and the restoration and maintenance of the just state. It must not only pray, it must act. And this means being willing to bear arms against injustice.

Similarly in his Gifford lectures in 1937–38, published as *The Knowledge of God and the Service of God* (Scribner), Barth outlines the conditions under which resistance to the state can be justified and even urged in Christian terms.

This brief historical review is given to dispel the common American stereotype that Barth's theology leads to ethical quietism. On the contrary, Barth has always been deeply involved in the ethical issues of his day, and his stand against Nazi tyranny, as we have just seen, was unequivocal. All of this was more than just a matter of political preference; it proceeded from the very heart and core of Barth's theology. Unfortunately, not too many American readers have delved very deeply into Barth's mammoth *Church Dogmatics,* of which seven "part-volumes" are now available in English. Suffice it to say that in this attempt to deal comprehensively with the Christian faith, Barth links dogmatics and ethics more closely than perhaps any other systematic theologian has ever done. The indissolubility of the two is inherent in his entire approach to dogmatics. The over-all way in which this relationship is established is spelled out in the latter half of *Church Dogmatics*, II, 2. In III, 4, he deals very explicitly with such matters as marriage, war, suicide, and a host of other ethical problems as they emerge from a study of the doctrine of creation. Volume IV, 3 (Zweite Hälfte), due this year, will engage in the same kind of grappling with the problem of the "calling." Barth's theology, then, is emphatically not one of lofty unconcern for the given ethical problems of man's specific situation, but precisely an attempt to show how at all points the gracious God relates himself to man's situation, and how man is to live in the light of the fact that the gracious God has done this.

Given, then, this central ethical thrust in Barth's theology, and given also the fact of his uncompromising and courageous opposition to Nazism throughout the Hitler regime, most people expected that at the conclusion of World War II Barth would turn his polemical sights on the "totalitarian" character of contemporary communism in almost exactly the same terms. With the change of a word here and there, Barth's anti-Nazi writings could presumably have been turned into almost equally effective anti-Communist writings.

But the fact of the matter is that these anticipations turned out to be quite ill-founded. Barth did not begin an attack on communism. He did not align himself with those who looked upon it as a menace to the future of Western civilization. In fact, partly goaded by Emil Brunner, who from a vigorously anti-Communist orientation publicly asked Barth again and again why he was so uncritical of communism, Barth began once more to turn out pamphlets and speeches and essays in which he took a very different line vis-à-vis communism from that which he had taken vis-à-vis Nazism. Fortunately for the American reader (though perhaps unfortunately in terms of getting a full picture of Barth's specifically political writings) a number of these essays are available in English, having been translated in the collection entitled *Against the Stream: Shorter Post-War Writings 1946-1952.*[2]

For our present purposes, it will be enough to highlight a few comments from "The Church between East and West," an article which first appeared in *Unterwegs* in 1949. Here Barth outlines some of the reasons why he is so unwilling to engage in the all-out offensive against communism which Brunner was urging upon him. He feels that the post-World War II struggle is basically a struggle between Russia and the United States. They are both children who have very suddenly grown up into giants. Each would like to master the other, and Europe is in the unhappy position of being a buffer between them.

[2] Published by Student Christian Movement Press, London, 1954. For a very full appraisal of Barth's attitude toward communism, cf. also Charles West, *Communism and the Theologians,* Westminster Press, Philadelphia, 1958, especially chaps. 5 and 6.

What, then, is to be "the Christian attitude" toward this conflict? Barth says that the answer can be simply put. First, "we must under no circumstances take fright" (p. 130). A single hymn by Paul Gerhardt is actually stronger than the worst things people can read in the papers about the American-Russian impasse. But secondly, and for our present purposes more important, the Christian is "not to take part in the conflict. As Christians it is not our concern at all. It is not a genuine, not a necessary, not an interesting conflict. It is a mere power-conflict" (p. 131). Barth rehearses the charges which America makes against Russia, and the charges which Russia makes against America, and decides that neither side is very convincing. So he exhorts his European Christian friends not to join "in the battle-hymn of the West." "It has pleased God," he continues, "to bring us into the world as men of the West. But it does not follow by any means that it pleases Him that we should simply give way to Western prejudices and especially to the pressure of our Western environment" (p. 135).

This does not mean joining the cause of the East. It means rather joining neither cause. The only possible way is a third way.

This essay was something of a bombshell to the churches of the West. Was this the Barth who had led the attack on Nazism? Was this the man who had seen the perils of totalitarianism so perceptively when they arose on German soil? What had happened? As if anticipating that this question would be raised,

Barth concludes his essay with an attempt to describe why the attitude toward communism must be different from what the attitude toward Nazism had been. He claims that the decision against Nazism was simple, and that one could say "no" with a clear conscience. But there are no simple repetitions in history, and the word against the Nazis is not by that token necessarily the word against anyone else. Barth also tries to discriminate between communism in practice and the communist ideology, a distinction he has attempted to maintain in other writings as well. He then launches into an attack on the West—a theme in his writings which has certainly been increasing in vigor rather than diminishing since 1949—and points out in effect that if the East is not very good, the West is not much better. One could be considerably more vigorous in one's opposition to communism, he feels, if Western democracy were appreciably better than communism:

> As long as there is still a "freedom" in the West to organize economic crises, a "freedom" to dump our corn into the sea here while people are starving there, so long as these things can happen, we Christians, at any rate, must refuse to hurl an absolute "no" at the East (p. 140).

There is another important difference for Barth between communism and Nazism. It is that communism makes no pretense at being Christian. One of the subtle lures of Nazism, Barth felt, was its attempt to present itself as a new form of salvation for the German people, with a new messiah, a new gospel, an eschatology, and all the rest. And many Christian pastors were willing to preach this gospel from their pulpits. Communism is not anti-Christian; it is simply and coldly non-Christian. It does not try to falsify or assimilate Christianity as Nazism did. It is brutally, but honestly, godless. Thus it does not pose the same kind of threat to the life and message of *the church* that Nazism did, and the church should not get exercised about it, since it is only one option in a power struggle which need not concern the church.

So for these and other reasons the church must stand neither against the West nor the East. "It can only walk between the two." The church's real task in this situation is to call all men back to humanity, and that will be its most important contribution to postwar reconstruction.

IV

Even this brief précis will make clear to the American reader that Barth has for some time been saying things which are most uncongenial to Western ears. We have become accustomed to insisting that a Christian must take a stand in the current world struggle, make a decision as between West and East; and that his decision, if he is free to make a real decision, will be a decision for the West. These are precisely

the things Barth refused to do in 1949, and they are
what he again refuses to do in 1959, as the *Letter to
a Pastor in the German Democratic Republic* makes
clear. In fact, the reader who has read *Against the
Stream* will perhaps wonder why there was so much
fuss about the East German letter when it first appeared, for in it Barth is saying substantially the same
things that he has been saying for a decade about
communism and about the struggle between East and
West.

Perhaps the significance of the East German letter
is mainly that it *has* come ten years later, and that in
that ten-year period the posture of world communism
has, to most people in the West, become clearer and
clearer. Probably the most notable event in that decade was the unsuccessful Hungarian uprising of October, 1956. Before this revolt, Barth had written in
somewhat glowing terms of the situation in Hungary
—at least he seems in retrospect to have been overly
sanguine about the Communist regime there. After
the Hungarian uprising, and the instances which it
provided of the brutality and terrorizing tactics of the
Communist regime, Reinhold Niebuhr asked, in
The Christian Century, "Why is Karl Barth Silent
about Hungary?" For whatever reasons, Barth kept
his silence, and the present East German letter makes
clear that the Hungarian uprising has not notice-
ably changed his appraisal of twentieth century
communism.

In 1948, a pastor in East Germany, writing on behalf of a group of his colleagues, wrote to Barth and asked him for counsel about the difficult task of proclaiming the gospel behind the Iron Curtain. In particular, he put eight specific questions to Barth and asked for his reactions. The now famous *Letter to a Pastor in the German Democratic Republic,* written at the end of August, 1958, was Barth's reply. We need not summarize this letter as fully as we did the essay by Hamel, for the letter is a much more "occasional" piece of writing and is more easily assimilated even after one reading. After only the briefest summary of its contents, we will make some comments upon it. The letter falls in four parts.[3]

First, Barth greets the East German pastor through whom the questions were asked, and gives a brief explanation of why he has not spoken a word to them before—an explanation we will discuss below.

Secondly, Barth devotes the main body of the letter to exhortation, counsel, and encouragement to his fellow Christians living in a difficult situation. This is a vigorous and compelling setting forth of a biblical basis for living in the midst of a time of troubles. This part of the document will have relevance long after the specific problems which prompted it have passed and have perhaps been replaced by other specific problems. Here again, as was true in the Hamel essay, we see how the forces of biblical faith can be

3 In the following paragraphs I am expanding material which appeared previously as "Barth's 'Letter to a Pastor in East Germany,'" in *Christianity and Crisis,* April 27, 1959, pp. 53–54. Used by permission.

related helpfully to specific and discouraging situations. The gospel remains true despite outward circumstances which seem to deny its truth. This is still
God's world despite all signs to the contrary. The
faith can speak to men in desperate circumstances
today just as it has spoken to men in desperate circumstances in former days. Barth makes a great deal
of 1 Peter 5:8-9:

> Be sober, be watchful. Your adversary the devil
> prowls around like a roaring lion, seeking someone
> to devour. Resist him, firm in your faith, knowing
> that the same experience of suffering is required of
> your brotherhood throughout the world.

Barth is concerned, quite rightly, to point out that
the "roaring lion" cannot *just* be equated with communism, and that to "resist" is not *just* to be an anti-
Communist. For the real "roaring lion," the real
devil, the real antichrist, may be much more difficult to distinguish, and the power of this adversary
may well be at work in the West in less discernible
forms than communism. Therefore, the manifestations of the "roaring lion" need to be resisted just as
much on the western side of the Iron Curtain as do
those manifestations of his presence which appear on
the eastern side.

What shines through this part of the letter is
Barth's positive faith in the gospel of God's sovereign
grace—the note which pervades volume after volume
of his *Church Dogmatics*. There is a joyfulness which

is possible in the service of God, wherever he has placed one. Since God is sovereign, the Christian can live in the assurance that God's purposes will endure and triumph, no matter how the events of the moment may seem to deny the strength of those purposes. The Christian should feel no regret that he is called upon to rely simply upon the Word and the Spirit. For these are the true weapons of his warfare, and the church resists, and is "firm in the faith," only when the faith of the church is *this* faith.

The third section of the letter consists of Barth's answers to the eight questions which were addressed to him. Here he offers quite specific (and quite debatable) advice, and it is from this section that most of the quotations in the American press releases were drawn. The reader who turns to this section will discover why. Here, for example, Barth seems to have no difficulty whatever in urging East German pastors to take the required loyalty oath to the East German Communist government—even though he doesn't know the precise content of the oath. Nor does he think it proper to try to "pray away" the Communist government, because the alternative might be the (apparently) worse fate of having to live under "the American way of life."

Finally, Barth offers a closing salutation, and urges the East German pastors to remember that those living in West Germany have their problems too, and that they have in their own way to cope with the "roaring lion" referred to in 1 Peter.

V

What are we to say about this document? Let us first of all point out some of the areas in which critical questions can be raised, and then go on to suggest some of the reasons why westerners can be grateful to Barth for this letter.

1. One must ask whether Barth does not perhaps purchase his vantage point above the struggle at too high a price. Can one really be permitted the luxury of refusing to make a choice—however discriminating and intelligent and qualified—between East and West? Is there really so little at stake in this struggle? Is not the Christian forced to involve himself a little more decisively in the kinds of decisions which may in the long run determine whether our civilization will be under Communist or democratic rule?

It is Barth's refusal to descend to this level of choice which so vexes a critic like Reinhold Niebuhr. He claims—and in terms of Barth's attitude concerning East and West, he claims with some justice—that Barth wants a "pure" choice before he commits himself. That is to say, if America and the West are not all Barth thinks they should be, he will remain neutral rather than align himself with a cause that may be somewhat tainted. Or, if Barth feels that communism does have certain unfortunate qualities, he will refuse to say so out loud, for fear of being used by the propaganda mill of the detestable westerners.

2. That these comments are made by an American will no doubt cause those of Barth's persuasion to discount them in advance. Such comments will seem to them a perfect example of the self-righteous attitude of Americans which they deplore. But I would assert that the question of whether or not there is a *significant* difference between East and West must be asked, and that it need *not* be asked self-righteously, but can be asked with a high measure of self-criticism. An American can acknowledge that there is a great deal wrong with American foreign policy, that American identification of its power with God's will is monstrously perverse, etc., etc., and still wonder whether Barth is in a position to speak quite so surely as he does about the utter chauvinism and moral flabbiness of America. Many readers have felt that Barth's political position is informed more decisively by being anti-American, than it is by being pro-anything. Here one can only wish that Barth had at some time in his life taken the trouble to know America at first hand. For political decisions, as Barth is elsewhere the first to acknowledge, must be based not only upon the Word of God but upon a solid respect for facts rather than fantasies.

3. Barth himself raises the question of his refusal to comment on the uprisings against communism in Hungary. But he simply resorts to *ad hominem* polemics of an unworthy sort in trying to explain why he kept silent. It is surely not unreasonable to have asked Barth for his reactions to the Hungarian situ-

ation in 1956, when he was so free with comments
about it in 1948 (see *Against the Stream,* pp. 51–124).
If words of praise are uttered when things seem to be
going well, and a dignified silence is maintained
when the cause becomes tarnished, observers are entitled to wonder whether the judgment of the gospel
on *all* aspects of human life is still being exercised,
or whether there are certain areas which the gospel
is not supposed to judge. At all events, Barth's feeling that Reinhold Niebuhr's question was an im-
proper question shows that America is not the only
place where one can become insulated from the fate-
ful day-to-day decisions men must make.

4. Specific criticisms could surely be raised about
Barth's answers to the eight detailed questions. He
wisely says in several places that he is not acquainted
with the East German situation at first hand, and that
therefore his answers may not be just what they
should be. But one wonders a bit at the confidence
with which he can then go on, from the isolation of
neutral Switzerland (and the Bernese Emmenthal at
that), to give such confident replies to men in situations which he has not experienced, where life and
death and moral integrity might well hang in the
balance if Barth's replies were taken seriously. One
must hope that in the cases where Barth did *not*
know the details of the situation, his answers did not
become wrong answers in the light of a true knowledge of those situations.

5. In conclusion we must raise once more a question that Karl Barth has surely answered for himself a hundred times. But the question persists: What are the basic reasons for the amazing shift of attitude from Nazism to communism? Granting all the things Barth says in earlier essays about American international irresponsibility, granting that America to a European seems much more menacing than Americans are able to understand, do not the moral indignities, the callous disregard for human life, the gradual warping of the original Communist ideology to fit the present Communist practice, the purges, the secret police, the rule of the few over the many—do not these and a dozen other realities of the communism of the 1950's make necessary a more penctrating kind of criticism than anything Karl Barth has yet offered us?

The above comments are typical of criticisms which have been raised since Barth's letter was first published. But it would be far too easy simply to offer these criticisms as though they thereby "disposed" of Barth's letter—or even of Barth. On the contrary, we must conclude by pointing out some of the reasons why we in the West can be grateful that Barth wrote his letter.

1. We have already commented on the fact that this letter is an attempt to let a word from the Bible speak to the world today. As is always the case in

Barth's theology, the message he proclaims is not primarily a word from man, though it is of course a word through man, but rather an honest attempt to find a word from the Lord. In this letter we have a stirring attempt to spell out what it means to affirm "God above all things." And we have an attempt to listen to a word of Scripture originally addressed to churches under persecution (1 Peter), and a word of Scripture originally addressed to the Jews in their time of captivity (Jeremiah 29). The bulk of the latter chapter is a letter from Jeremiah to the Jews who are in exile under Nebuchadnezzar in Babylon. The following verses are typical of the advice he gives them:

> Build houses and live in them; plant gardens and eat their produce. Take wives and have sons and daughters; take wives for your sons, and give your daughters in marriage, that they may bear sons and daughters; multiply there, and do not decrease. But seek the welfare of the city where I have sent you into exile, and pray to the Lord on its behalf, for in its welfare you will find your welfare (Jeremiah 29:5-7).

Thus it will be seen that much of the advice that Barth gives to the East Germans is simply an attempt to let a relevant word from Scripture be heard today.

The question, of course, can still be raised: Is *this* the relevant word from Scripture? Why this passage and not some other? Surely Barth would not have thus counseled—and did not in fact counsel—Christians who were under Nazi persecution to behave in this way. This question is no new question, and it need not be addressed only to Barth. It is the question which must always haunt the Christian who is seeking to see life through biblical eyes: *Which* portion of Scripture speaks most clearly to my situation today?

2. A second helpful thing that we gain from this letter is a clearer insight into why Barth has been so loath to raise his voice against contemporary communism. Aside from certain personal reasons, such as the desire to press on to the completion of his *Dogmatics,* Barth points out that to speak a word against communism means almost immediately being picked up and used by anti-Communists of the crudest sort, and transformed against one's will into an uncritical and holy crusader for the West. We have already noted that Barth may be asking for more here than history is ever going to give him, but we in America must still feel the force of his charge. Our anti-communism, however justified on some levels it may be, is usually clothed with a self-righteous pro-Americanism which is certainly impossible to justify in the light of the gospel. Barth may be wrong in assuming that this entitles him to avoid "taking sides," but he is surely right in cringing before the unholy alliance between America and God's will which seems to result if he does.

Furthermore, Barth is at least not quite so blind to evils under Communist regimes as some of his critics have assumed. He says, "I disapprove just as much the spirit and the words, the methods and the practices of the system under which you live [i.e., in East Germany] as I do the powers and dominions that rule over us here in the West." This may not sound like much of a concession to Western ears, but it is more than many critics of Barth had ever led us to believe would be forthcoming.

3. It may sound strange to say so at first, but we need to thank Karl Barth for his very harsh words about the West, and even for his comparison of "the fleshpots of Egypt" and "the American way of life." Whether we think this is either fair or accurate, it is a fact that Barth and many other Europeans see America in precisely these terms. We are not entitled to assume that this picture is merely the product of the distorted imagination of the persons who are looking at us. We must be ready to acknowledge that there is some relationship between what we are and what the Europeans see when they look at us. Americans do not like to admit such things but it behooves us to do so, not merely in a kind of public acknowledgement of guilt, but with intent to repent. In speaking of us as sharply as he does, Barth says a word we need to hear, for he describes the image of ourselves which we have projected on the rest of the world. And we are not entitled to take the easy out of saying that Barth's picture is such a caricature as

to be irrelevant. Even a caricature can convey a needed truth.

4. In more positive terms, Barth says an important word to the West in warning all his readers that the "roaring lion" does not just exist behind the Iron Curtain. Evil in the twentieth century is not embodied solely in communism. Evil in the twentieth century may be even more dangerous in its more subtle forms, those forms of evil which masquerade as good. It may even prove to be the case, for example, that in the long sweep of history American self-righteousness will have more baleful effects on mankind than the overt evil which communism represents. Americans would no doubt find it hard to be persuaded of this possibility—and yet the very strangeness of the notion to Americans may simply be a further indication of the subtle force of evil at work in the West. Those in the West, Barth reminds his brethren in the East, "must withstand an 'adversary,' though in an entirely different disguise, as well as they can, and must prove their solidarity with you in doing it."

". . . their solidarity with you . . ." A solidarity between East and West as they confront a common adversary in differing guises! Let the West remember this—we, too, face an adversary, and we, too, need to be strengthened for battle. And the one who thinks that the adversary is *only* communism will already have lost the battle, for he will have blinded himself to the possibility of seeing the adversary that exists within his own heart.

VI

So we learn many things—both pro and con—from Barth's letter. Let the last thing be a recognition that Christians may quite legitimately disagree when it comes to their specific political decisions. If one thinks that Barth has made mistakes here, let him profit from the mistakes. But whatever the specific political decisions may be, let every reader learn from Barth that he, too, in his own situation, is called upon to do what Barth does—to read the Bible hopefully and expectantly, eagerly believing that God will bring forth yet more truth from his Word.

LETTER TO A PASTOR
IN THE GERMAN DEMOCRATIC REPUBLIC

by Karl Barth

Dear Unknown and Well-known One!

Your letter, accompanied by what you wrote to our mutual friend, reached me, and I have read it more than once with great sympathy and attention. You wish to hear from me something about your situation and your problems. You have furnished me with an informative account (on which I will not directly comment in the following, for reasons known to you). Finally, you have approached me with eight concrete questions.

"Why doesn't Karl Barth say a guiding word also to us?" Let me first deal with this question which you addressed to our mutual friend. It reminds me for a moment of a "why?" which was posed to me publicly by a well-known American theologian just two years ago, when the East-West storm was raging fiercely for us here. "Why is Karl Barth Silent about

Hungary?" At that time I didn't say a single word in answer, for obviously it was not an honest question. It was not inspired by the real distress of a Christian seeking genuine conversation and fellowship with another, but it was addressed to me by a hard-boiled politician safe in his castle. He, as is customary with politicians who lead an opponent onto slippery ice, wished either to force me to profess his own brand of primitive anti-communism, or to expose me as a secret pro-Communist, and thus in one way or another discredit me as a theologian. What should I have said to that? Your question—though I detect even in it a faint trace of ill will—is of a quite different sort. In any case, you ask from a place where the sterile *anti* or *pro* can play only an insignificant role, since where you are you must come to grips daily with the reality of communism and, whatever the cost, make the best of it. You fear, in your own words, "nothing more than a liberation according to Adenauer's ideas, which would lead us back to the flesh-pots of Egypt." You evaluate the socialism of your country as a respectable attempt to cultivate something new and, as you wish for it a healthy, free development, you are not led astray by the gloomy predictions of the West German radio. To be sure, you then list a number of harsh facts which cause trouble for you as a pastor and a Christian in the East Zone. And you want me to think through the meaning of these facts with stark realism and to give you my counsel. You approach me, trusting that I may be capable of this, capable of saying to you a "fatherly," a "guiding," and even a "liberating" word that will "make you glad." I wonder whether what I can say will partake of these high qualities even just a bit? This much is certain: when a man questions me as you do, I can, I must, and I want to try to answer as well as it is in my power.

First of all, why have I not done this long ago? I know very well why not! For one thing, it is because, as time goes on, I like less and less to discuss a matter unless both outer necessity and inner necessity compel me to say something definite. Up to now, no one has required me so explicitly and compellingly, as you have just done, to say something regarding the problem of Christian existence under God in the German East Zone. Furthermore, one would need to have spent all these years with you, to have experienced in one's own life the growing pressure under which you stand. One would need to have tried out personally the various possibilities of withstanding it, in order to avoid coming up with some kind of wisdom which, because of a deficient knowledge of the facts, situations, and persons, might be totally irrelevant to your questions. Moreover I confess to you that rather than give you advice from afar, I would ten times prefer to learn to my own edification and instruction what good people in your own ranks are writing on the subject. I think at the moment of the excellent essay which Johannes Hamel contributed to the *Thurneysen-Festschrift*, which appeared this

summer under the title "The Proclamation of the
Gospel in the Marxist World." "You have Moses and
the prophets," I might have exclaimed with Father
Abraham; "what more do you need?" Furthermore,
fifteen or twenty-five years ago I still had enough
breath to write *Church Dogmatics* with my right
hand and give various "guiding words" with my left:
first concerning the *Kirchenkampf*, the struggle of
the Confessing Church against Hitler's Germany;
then to stir up and sustain my Swiss countrymen
when they were threatened in 1940 with "weak
knees"; and lastly for the benefit of the oppressed
Christians in France, Holland, and elsewhere. But
today I have neither the time nor the energy to do
both. Were I forced to choose between the two, I am
inclined to think that Christians on both sides of the
Iron Curtain will be better served on the whole if
instead of making direct pronouncements, I do what
I am yet given to do for the *Dogmatics*. Finally, I
should like just to whisper in your ear, if that were
possible, one more reason for my past silence that
dare not be missing from the list. How can I write
to you without revealing that I disapprove just as
much the spirit, and the words, the methods, and
the practices of the system under which you live, as
I do the powers and dominions that rule over us here
in the West? I would find it quite bearable that such
an exposure might easily lose me the little glory of
being counted among the "progressive theologians"—
a reputation which I have so far enjoyed in many

places in East Germany. But how can I speak my
mind without unwillingly casting all kinds of fuel in
the fire of anti-communism which flares up glaringly
enough in our part of the world and no doubt constantly glimmers in yours? How could I avoid being
praised and used by people whom I consider to be
notoriously the worst enemies of all truth, all justice,
and all peace? But enough of this. All these arguments have their obvious weaknesses. I will put them
aside this once, give my heart a push, and, moved by
what you have written to me, say what I think.

The First Epistle of Peter, I should think, is a portion of the New Testament that today is read with
special attentiveness in the East German Republic by
all who want to be true Christians. In that epistle,
the churches are challenged to "resist . . . firm in
faith" (5:9). To resist whom? "Your adversary, the
devil," says the passage, "who prowls around like a
roaring lion, seeking some one to devour." The author certainly had in mind some very concrete difficulty, temptation, and danger that was threatening
the members of these churches. To many of you in
East Germany—and to the more of you, the nearer
you live to the western boundary—the "adversary"
is probably communism, which in its specifically German and therefore thorough and consistent form
looks like an especially fierce and ravening lion. Still,
to identify that "lion" with communism as such is to
fall into the trap of a dangerous optical illusion.
Those who make this identification straightway con-

clude that the "resistance" of the Christian is opposition to communism. In other words, Christian resistance is to take the form of an openly or subtly
active "anti-communism."

The matter, however, is more complicated. Of
course, communism as such has something, and not
just a little, to do with that "adversary," but to be
exact, only insofar as it has the form and power of a
tempter who can seduce and mislead men (and especially Christian people) into anxiety, blind submission, blind hate, indecision, and double-talk, into
serpentine wisdom from dovelike simplicity, into
howling with the wolves or fear of being eaten by
them, into collaboration or obstructionism, worry,
and the subsequent use of all false means and
weapons to which care-ridden mortals are accustomed
to resort. In short, into that godlessness in action
which is truly atheism. Where and insofar as communism thus misleads and seduces men—and only
there and only insofar—is it to be identified with the
lion that prowls the East today. Communism that
would willfully create this ruin is to be resisted.

But the New Testament passage, as it continues,
affirms that Christians who are tempted in this particular way should consider "that the same sufferings
befall your brotherhood throughout the world."
Since you write me that you fear nothing so much as
"liberation according to Adenauer's ideas," I venture to assume that we are agreed on the matter
which I should like to discuss next. The roaring lion

has other, no less threatening forms besides the one in which he seems to meet you in the East. You probably know that the people in the sixteenth century spoke of the Turks and the Pope as of an Eastern and a Western antichrist. I prefer not to use that term either for the Eastern or the Western power. Nor, for that matter, did I want to have it used for Hitler in his time. I conceive of the "antichrist" as more inspiring and more inviting, because friendlier and more convincing in character than the Pope or the Turks of the sixteenth century, the wretched Hitler, or the two contemporary antagonists. The real antichrist will be much more difficult to distinguish from Christ than any of these; in fact, he will be a kind of Christ-figure. Who knows, he may in some way resemble the meek and mild representation of Christ like that of Thorwaldsen. Such great ultimate words should certainly be used with more restraint than is likely to be the case in the heat of controversy. I recall those earlier antagonists because one thing is certain: one cannot interpret the particular behavior and activity of the contemporary Eastern power in whose realm you live as representing the one and only embodiment of the prowling adversary of Christianity. The present-day Western power has at least this one point in common with the Eastern, that it too, in its own way, seeks to dissuade the Christian Church from being the church. It attempts to silence the fearless, resounding proclamation so alien and so disturbing to the world, that God's rule is close at hand and will ultimately be revealed to the whole earth, that his kingdom is supreme and victorious over all economic, political, ideological, cultural, and also religious realms of life.

You speak several times in your letter of your government's obviously increasing "hostility to Christ." This might be so, although this remains an open question. In any event such a "hostility" exists not only in the Communist East but also in the so-called "free" West, though in a different guise. You clearly know that. But you must reckon with this truth and keep it before your eyes day in and day out. The church's message of Christ as the sum and substance of this coming reign is just as repugnant and embarrassing to the West as it is to the East. Who knows, perhaps it is even *more* repugnant and *more* embarrassing to the West. An adverse spirit and power is mightily at work against this testimony not only in the East, but also in the West; not only in the avowed totalitarianism in which you live, but also in the creeping totalitarianism in which we live. In the East there is arbitrary rule of the almighty party, propaganda, and police, but in the West we are surrounded by an equally tyrannous press, systems of private enterprise, snobbish presumption, and public opinion. For the sake of the church's witness it is as necessary here as there to "resist . . . firm in the faith." Anyone who fails to resist the Western lion with all his might will certainly not be able, either, to resist the Eastern lion. Indeed such a person doesn't know

what he is talking about when he speaks of a "lion."
It may be that we lack just as much as you do the
necessary imagination to see clearly what the required resistance concretely means for the Christian
on the other side of the fence. But we must trust each
other's word that it is exceedingly difficult for the
church and for individual Christians here and there to
find and to tread ever again the narrow path of obedience, to resist on both sides the compulsory domesti-
cation and, even more, the ever-present temptation to
voluntary conformism. We must also know how hard
it is to refrain from sterile opposition and defiance
and to remain unswervingly faithful to the gospel of
free grace, valid yet strange and unpopular among
us as among you. The burden that is thus laid upon
you may look very different from ours. We must
nevertheless recognize it as the *one* burden inevitably
to be borne by the one Church of Jesus Christ, by all
of us together. But 1 Peter and the rest of the New
Testament are equally insistent on sharing the joy
that is assured to all who have to shoulder that
burden. Christians in the East German Republic are
herewith informed that we are no less in need of their
concern for us and their rejoicing with us than they
are of ours.

Now don't be angry with me if I go on to state
a homely truth: the only thing you and I can do in the
grip of tribulation and anxiety is to lay hold again
of the *prima et ultima ratio,* to practice the ABC's
of the Christian faith. Simply put, to believe truly

and gladly in the God as whose witnesses we are commissioned, you there and we here. To believe in him means, as you know as well as I do, to fear and love him, his kingdom and his grace above all else, and so to fear and love our Lord and Savior Jesus Christ above all things; to acknowledge him and submit to him in all our problems, great and small, as the One who was, is, and is to come; to risk everything in our personal and in our corporate life on the faith that he will provide all that is good for us, and that all he provides will be good. This belief is, even in the East German Republic, the only key, the only treasure, the only armor. But there as well as here it *is* the one key, the one treasure, the one armor beyond compare. God above all things! In the light of what you have written me, I want to try to interpret and apply this truth.

God above all things! He is the One who has willed and ordained that the Christian Church be both confident and joyful in the midst of mankind to have a gift and a task even under the domination of an alien power, a socialism that is inspired and directed by Moscow! An alien power? Yes, but not only an alien power. This power in all its characteristics can be but God's instrument, inescapably fulfilling a function in his plan. The judicial function of a rod of discipline? Yes, even this function. This power would not have gained control over you had it not been for all the sins of past leaders and people in society, state, and church. You are assuredly undergoing a painful

process of purification and fiery refining, such as the
Western world also will not escape sooner or later in
some form, perhaps at the hands of Asia and Africa.
But who sits in judgment? Not the instrument, but
the One who uses it and holds it in his hand, the gracious and merciful One who even when he is angry
and punishes, and especially then, does not desire that
anyone be lost, but that all, Christians and non-Christians, be saved and come to the knowledge of the
truth. He judges only because he loves us and in order
to bless us. Is there any hope for a turn for the better
in your brand of socialism? Why not? But the West
German radio might also be right with its mumbling
and grumbling that nowhere is hope in sight. Nevertheless, hope in God is not in vain, even under the
rule of socialism—over which he reigns as well, using
it to further his work. The Christian Church in the
East Zone of Germany might now be gathered as a
people that rests its hope in God alone, without illusion or reticence or complaint, putting us all to shame
and at the same time encouraging us. Sooner or later
this people of God will surely have reasons, large or
small, for thankfulness. Perhaps, as you hint, it already has such reasons.

But far better than anything I can say to you about
your basic attitude to the alien power that over-
shadows you is what the prophet Jeremiah, in the
29th chapter of his book, writes to the exiled He-
brews in Babylon. I cannot urge you strongly enough

to read this chapter with care, as if for the first time, and to let what is said there speak to you in your situation in spite of all other considerations.

God above all things! Sovereign even over atheism and materialism, which your state really seems to carry to excess. I am familiar enough with the big textbook full of pictures which begins with the nebulae and ends with the portraits of Karl Marx, Lenin, and, in my copy, still with Stalin. But God is sovereign also over theories! Or do you think that those theories could actually hurt the living God, or even a single person, whether child or adult, educated or uneducated? It would take more than a little or even a great deal of materialism, especially when one considers how for a long enough time we have been carrying our pernicious idealism to excess! Don't be alarmed. The bubble of a genuine and equally pernicious materialism will burst at the appointed time, as the bubble of idealism had to burst when its time came. The "masterpieces" of your court-poets will not be able to alter the course of events at all. And what about atheism? Don't you think that most of what calls itself atheism is to be taken seriously only insofar as it has arisen from misunderstandings caused by the prevailing teaching, attitudes, and practices of the Christian Church? I am reminded of a delightful but thought-provoking anecdote which I heard recently. One Berliner confesses to another that he has now left the Church. "So you don't believe in God?" the other replies. "In God, yes," the first answers, "but not in his ground-crew." It is not as a rule the fault of the "ground-crew," of us Christians in general and of us theologians in particular, that people come to consider and announce themselves as atheists? All they can deny is the existence of a conceptual idol with which they are familiar, not the life and work of the eternal God whom they do not know, though he knows them all the better. Do they think that he, who in Jesus Christ has accepted all men, including them, would become "a-human" because some people dare to think that they can become "a-theistic"? As though they could thereby escape him! As though we were permitted as Christians to believe that such people had succeeded or could succeed in escaping him, or that they had the power to wrest others out of his hand! If you want my advice, it can only be this: in principle and in practice you should accept none of your countrymen at their own estimate. Don't ever honor them as the unbelieving and strong men they pretend to be! (As a matter of fact such customers are not only found in the Communist East.) They are just posing as the strong men they would like to be! Rather, you must meet their unbelief with a joyous unbelief in their attempted atheism. You as Christians must confidently claim that your atheists belong to God as much as you do. Whether they will be converted (or indeed whether you will convert them) may be more doubtful; but this is a secondary question. What is certain is that

God is not against them, but for them. And you, for your part, not only may but must believe this for their sake and in their behalf. There is a sound basis on which you may live with these "enemies of Christ," who know not what they do: the basis for you to stand and to bear witness to them of the Lord who died and rose again for them also. To do otherwise, you would become an unbeliever, an atheist, and an enemy of Christ yourself.

God above all things! Sovereign even over the legalistic totalitarianism of your state! You fear it? Fear it not! The limits of that system where its representatives must halt or else be destroyed is set not by its totalitarianism, but by its legalism which makes the state totalitarian in an ungodly and inhuman way. "Totalitarian" also, in a way, is the grace of the gospel which we all are to proclaim, free grace, truly divine and truly human, claiming every man wholly for itself. To a degree the Communist state might be interpreted and understood as an image of grace— to be sure, a grossly distorted and darkened image. Indeed, grace is all-embracing, *totalitarian*. But it is totalitarian *grace* as free and freeing action and not as law; not as a spider's web of theses and antitheses, and surely not coercingly pressing for their recognition and realization, or overwhelming and crushing opposition wherever it appears—and where would that not be? The grace of the gospel, free in its divinity and in its humanity, conquers, overpowers, and rules from within outward and not vice versa. It does

not demand, it gives. It does not retaliate, it forgives.
It does not oppress, it lifts up. It does not stir up
wrath and it does not kill; it heals, binds up wounds,
provides like the Good Samaritan. Under the law
even that which is good, even that which is best, will
inevitably be changed into evil—as constantly happens in the East and in the West. Under grace, even
the evil can turn out only for the good, indeed for
the best. Do you believe in God's free grace? Of
course you do. Then you must be able to discern
the decisive weakness of the system under which you
live (and of ours as well), which resides in its legalism. God's superiority, then, is plain for you to see
at this point and casts out all fear. This means, of
course, that you will scrupulously avoid encountering
and counteracting your rulers on the ground unfortunately chosen by them, that is, merely countering
their crude ungodliness and inhumanity with more
refined versions of the same. They evidently fail (as
do the rulers on this side of the Iron Curtain) to
grasp a truth which we may not have made sufficiently clear to them: the Church of Jesus Christ in
the totalitarianism of her gospel confronts them on
an altogether different ground. The church cannot,
and indeed dare not, retaliate, returning measure for
measure. Were she to follow the rule of "an eye for
an eye," she would cease to be the salt of the earth
and the light of the world which she is intended to
be, not to mention the fact that she would never
succeed in the attempt. She is not to develop an

ecclesiastical legalism as over against a materialistic
legalism. She is not to rebut a materialistic world-
view with a Christian world-view. She has no Christian counterproposal to socialist mores and politics;
no episcopal or synodal-presbyterial official authority
to match the authority of police and party; no magic
of her own whereby to counter the monotonous
Marxist litany, the mass demonstrations, and the
slogans of communism. She would feel no regret that
she has to rely solely on the Word and the Spirit.
Undismayed, she can only set out ever afresh from
this point of departure, and ever again return to it:
love is the fulfillment of the law, and love achieves
the good which inevitably eludes all men who live
only by the law. Only "firm in the faith," that is in
this faith, can the church resist; never, in the name
or in honor of any principles or dogmas, in an attempt to compel anyone to recognize them in theory
or practice. She can only follow Jesus. Never in the
hour and place of her confrontation can she fix her
eyes on any other than the God of grace and the man
to whom he is gracious, on the God who is free and
the man who is to be set free by him. Then, whether
she speaks well or badly, she must speak clearly, call
clearly, and act decisively—questioning, warning,
comforting. At one time she will have openly to confess her faith. At another time she will maintain an
eloquent silence and stand aside. But always she will
be serving God and man, and thus will never be able
or willing to act as though she had both God and

man at her disposal. To "resist" in this way is certainly what the church must never forego among you and among us. And in just this way her resistance will always be firm, genuine, and first and last by no means ineffectual. Whether or not her witness will be believed, she will at any rate be worthy of belief, since she herself lives from faith. What you and we must fear and love above all things is not any abstract idea, theory, deity, or law, but God's free grace alone, eternally sovereign and revealed to us in Jesus Christ.

But he, God, and his free grace, is really above all thoughts, concepts, and usual practices by which we Christians ourselves in East and West have been accustomed to live, seemingly serving both the glory of God and the salvation of man! What a multitude of things we have taken for granted: a church occupying a comfortable place in the social structure, her existence guaranteed, or at least respected, or at the very least tolerated by society in general and by the state in particular! Sunday as a recognized holiday and day of rest, and the chief church festivals which have somehow left their impact on the life of the people as a whole; infant baptism, confirmation, marriage, and burial, the Christian landmarks of the milieu and the existence of Mr. Everyman—means whereby the church has liked to reassure herself again and again of her obvious indispensability! The influence of the church in public education, instruction and upbringing of young people; with the maximum claim that schools by right be Christian schools,

or with the minimum claim that they be not openly
opposed to "Christianity"! The prestige or at least
the dignity of her official representatives among the
leaders of other social and cultural organizations!
The formal recognition of the church's freedom to
participate in the discussion of general human concerns as a direct or indirect partner, welcome or un-
welcome! Although these privileges of Christianity
have never and nowhere gone unchallenged, certainly
not in the last few centuries, it has seemed to us the
most natural thing in the world that the proclamation of the gospel of Jesus Christ should continue to
run in some such channels as these, and that we
should do the utmost for their preservation and defense, for the sake of God and the gospel! And we
have done this zealously and repeatedly, both skill-
fully and unskillfully, successfully and unsuccessfully.
Were we not motivated by the assumption that the
Christian cause and confession can and must be
formally understood and appreciated in the normal
order of things by each and every citizen, at the very
least in terms of the free practice of "religion"? Is the
world as such obligated to grant to Christianity the
right to maintain that form of existence in its midst?
What is happening to your situation in the East
German republic, and possibly in other Marxist-
oriented lands, seems to cancel this whole bill of
rights. The same thing will probably happen to us
here in the West. With you it is no longer possible
to overlook the fact that it is happening. In the so-

cialist conception of the world and of man which powerfully asserts itself in your country, this brand of Christianity is gradually squeezed out. The time seems near or at least not far when the church in this form of existence will no longer have any place at all. The church will be foreign, despised and greatly suspect in the eyes of state and society. Membership in the church and confession of Christian faith will greatly jeopardize life's opportunities for individuals from school age onward. Your freedom of movement will be restricted to a minimum, and all that you are commissioned to do as a church will be done only in corners, in the shadow, with constant interference, harassment, and sabotage from without. The *Volkskirche* or National Church in the sense of the "Church of the people" will be only a dream.

It may be that the plight is not yet as bad as this in the East Zone, and that there are forces at work which are still counteracting this development. But the fact that this development is so obviously favored by your rulers is sufficient to beg questions in your minds as in ours: Can Christianity truly fulfill its task only in that form of existence which until now has been taken for granted? Only in the light of that public assistance, recognition, or at least tolerance? Only with the help of the whole apparatus of a national church and on the premise of freedom of action? Only as one strong pillar among others in the social structure? Only when it possesses a legal claim on each and every citizen? Just exactly where does

one read of the first churches of Jesus Christ in Jerusalem, Rome, Corinth, or Asia Minor as being permitted to enjoy this mode of existence? And where
are they promised it for some later time? Where do
we learn that its origin was in itself a good thing, or
that the church stands and falls with it, or that the
church is committed to it, come hell or high water?
I am not saying anything new to you in reference
to this question. It was indeed one of your most re-
nowned and ablest men, General Superintendent
Günther Jacob in Cottbus, who not long ago announced the "end of the Constantinian era." Because
I have a certain wariness about all theoretical formu-
lations of a philosophy of history, I hesitate to make
this expression my own. But it is certain that something resembling this approaching end begins to show
itself dimly everywhere, but very sharply in your part
of the world.

It is certain that we all have reason to ask ourselves each of these questions, and in every case
quickly and clearly to give the answer: No, the
church's existence does not always have to possess the
same form in the future that it has possessed in the
past, as though this were the only possible pattern.
No, the continuance and victory of the cause of God,
which the Christian Church is to serve with her witness, is not unconditionally linked with the forms
of existence which it has had until now. Yes, the hour
may strike and has perhaps already struck when God,
to our discomfiture, but to his glory and for the sal-

vation of mankind, will put an end to this mode of existence because it lacks integrity and has lost its usefulness. Yes, it could be our duty to free ourselves inwardly from our dependency on that mode of existence even while it still lasts. Indeed, on the assumption that it may one day entirely disappear, we definitely should look about us for new ventures in new directions.

Yes, as the Church of God we may depend on it that if only we are attentive, God will show us such new ways as we can hardly anticipate now. And as the people who are bound to God we may even now claim unconquerable security for ourselves through him. For his name is above all names, even above the name that we in human, all too human, fashion have hitherto borne in his service and in a kind of secular forgetfulness, confused with his own. Might it not be, dear brothers and sisters in the imperiled East Zone, that you there and we here are now to do justice to the old *Soli Deo Gloria* in an entirely new spirit of humility, openness, and readiness? Might it not be your special calling to be a living example for the rest of us of how a church lives that seeks for and perhaps has already entered upon a new way, of a church *for,* not of, the people—the church in "God's beloved (deeply beloved!) East Zone"?

*　　*　　*　　*

I now address myself to the eight specific questions you asked. You will understand that here I can speak only in part with the same definiteness which was possible in the foregoing discussion of the main issue. To say something useful to you here, I would need to have been with you in the thick of things, in order to understand exactly how your questions are meant and not meant. It would be better if we met face to face. You must excuse me in advance if I, even with the best intentions, should go a little astray in the fog. By the way, am I wrong in my impression that not all of these questions are your own, but that other persons, presumably your colleagues, have put in their word? However this may be, I will try to do my best.

1. Is the secret longing of the heart for German reunification patterned after Western prosperity and freedom exclusively to be reckoned as disobedience to the gospel?

Answer: Such a longing is certainly understandable and not at all without reason. Were I in your place, I think that I myself would feel the same longing very keenly. Life in the West doubtless has many advantages, and among them some very real ones. And it would be impossible, in the light of certain events at the borderline between the two German zones, to deny that life in the East has its notorious disadvantages. What counts is how much scope and importance you give to that longing in comparison

with your obedience to the gospel. The two can
hardly be identical. Or have you ever met a Christian
who impressed you as being wholly obedient to the
gospel in that he nourished this longing in his heart
or even let it materialize? If you distinguish between
this longing and the voice of the gospel, then you will
show your absolute obedience to the latter by giving
it the first place, and giving the other voice only a
second or third or fourth place in the order of your
thinking, willing, and doing. Not that you feel this
longing, but that you give it precedence over your
commitment to the gospel, is what would be reckoned "exclusively as disobedience."

2. *Can we pledge the required loyalty oath to the
East German government, in spite of the inherent
dangers?*

Answer: I don't know the exact wording of this
loyalty oath. I assume it is unlike the Hitler oath
("I vow fidelity and obedience to the Führer"), when
the one who pledged it had to buy a pig in a poke.
The content of the oath under consideration, I sup-
pose, is with the definition of the established form
of government, the essence of which is known to him
on the basis of the Constitution of the East German
Republic. (In the following I have Romans 13 in
mind, but also my own relation to the form of government of the Swiss Confederation as defined in its
constitution!) "Loyalty" to this established order
means honest readiness to recognize its existence and

to take one's place in it, perhaps assuming, but ignoring in practice, certain scruples caused by the "inherent dangers." "Loyalty" does *not* mean approval of the ideology on which this government is built. It does not mean approval of each and every measure of the actual officials and representatives of this government. "Loyalty" reserves the right of freedom of thought over against the ideology, and the right of opposition, even of resistance to particular implications and applications of the given system. There is such a thing as a loyal opposition. He is "loyal" to a given form of government who recognizes its validity and authority for himself and is resolved to accept it within the limits of what is inwardly and outwardly possible for him. I would not see any difficulty, were I in your shoes, in offering this loyalty to the East German Republic, and thus in truthfully pledging the oath that is required from you.

3. One of our theological teachers once maintained that the "silent of the land" prayed away the Third Reich. Would a similar prayer be allowed us in our present situation?

Answer: That report does not make me too happy because, as I have read in the biography of Kravielitzki, the respected head of a religious community and of an order of deaconesses, some of the "silent of the land" were at first exceedingly co-operative in ushering in the Third Reich. Whether you should co-operate in a possible present-day attempt to "pray away" the East German Republic depends upon whether or not you can seriously and responsibly come before the Lord with such a prayer. Would you not be afraid that he might hear and answer you in a terrible way? Could you not awake some morning amidst the "fleshpots of Egypt" and committed to the "American way of life"? Would you not find it more fruitful to pray *for* the East German Republic instead of against it and, for the rest, to beseech the Lord for light and strength to live and act in a truly Christian way right where you are?

4. To what extent can the curtailment of the church's right to the freedom to speak out and receive a public hearing be a reason for resistance, considering the fact that this is one of the major bases from which anti-Communist propaganda is launched?

Answer: The concept of the "church's right to the freedom to speak out and receive a public hearing" is in itself highly problematic. Only God himself can properly claim this freedom for his Word. The church has no "right" to make such a claim for her own word. The Word of God has a right to the faithful, accurate, and entirely unacclaimed service of the church's word. The freedom to speak out and receive a public hearing can only be granted to the church as a gift of God's free grace. The "curtailment" of the church's freedom ought therefore to be understood clearly as a divine work of love, carried out by the socialist state against its will, a work which it is not advisable to resist. The "anti-Communist propaganda" is launched from very shaky grounds indeed, theologically speaking, when it has chosen this as its major base.

5. The tense situation grates on our nerves and badly affects our inner condition. Irritations that border on heart failure literally lead to almost irreconcilable differences. Therefore, in spite of the compelling urgency of these and similar questions, can we still afford such endurance tests? Is it not our duty at times of greatest stress to be more concerned with the strategy for maintaining the inner solidarity of the church than with making our own better knowledge prevail?

Answer: This question causes me to tremble. Even to one who can care only from afar, it speaks so clearly and directly of what it means to be humanly and personally involved in the situation. I think I see how things get on your nerves and then affect your inner life. You and your brothers, threatened even with heart failure, fall out with each other in mutual irritation. How can I say anything helpful at this point when I would almost need to consult a physician for advice? If I can be useful at all, it is perhaps in regard to the alternative you suggest in your question. You ask whether, faced with the "endurance tests" occasioned by the discussion of the four preceding questions (and maybe also of those yet to come), you should count it more important to secure the recognition of your own better knowledge or to maintain a strategy for inner solidarity among Christian brothers. You seem to incline to the second solution. It seems to me that the alternative is not rightly stated. If Christians, pastors, and theologians are not united among themselves, then neither the question of "making your own better knowledge prevail" nor the one of the "inner solidarity" is of more than secondary importance, no matter how earnestly they present themselves. The real alternative must be as follows: In confronting these questions, are we willing to begin, all of us together, with the ABC's of what makes a Christian truly a Christian, forgetting at first the question as to the better knowledge of each individual and the concern for finding and preserving community of knowledge, but remaining constantly open? Are we willing to return once more to the Word of God, which concerns and commits us all, and to which we are all commissioned to bear witness? Are we willing to take stock of what the gospel of his free grace has to say to us and to our congregations here and now? Or are we for some reason unwilling to do that? Are we willing to read the previously mentioned 29th chapter of Jeremiah with unprejudiced openness and let it speak to us? Or do we find ourselves unready to do it? Submit to *these* "endurance tests," first each of you in his own study, and then all together in your meetings, and see what happens! Perhaps there will be some broken pieces. Perhaps a lot of what has seemed to be one's "better knowledge" is really not worth "prevailing" and will be flung to the dogs. Perhaps much of what is thought to be "solidarity," but really is weak and corrupted or to be gained only by the sacrifice of integrity, will be discarded. It is certain that by this procedure you will arrive at a new and more useful knowledge, and then also at a new and more genuine solidarity. It is also certain that the other alternative will either disappear or, as is appropriate, become relative. And it is certain—I believe I may be allowed to make this prediction without being a doctor—that *these* "endurance tests" will ease your nerves so that they will no longer worry you, and the heart failure which has been threatening all of you will be counteracted in a healthy way. But what am I saying here? "The Word, the Word, the Word must do it," all along the line. In fact, the Word *will* do it.

6. *Is not self-defense of the church also laid upon us, since otherwise we could lose the only sphere where the gospel can be freely proclaimed? Does not the admonition of the "peace pastors" "to invade the world with the love of Christ" serve finally only those who want to rob us of the opportunity to proclaim the gospel?*

Answer: After what I have said earlier, you will certainly be able to anticipate what I have to say to this question. I cannot believe that the church is permitted, let alone commissioned, to practice self-defense any more than she has a legal claim to the freedom to speak out and get a public hearing. She may in good confidence expect the state and society to grant her such "opportunity to proclaim the gospel," and if it is granted, gratefully to make use of it. However, she does not possess a right to such opportunity; and to proclaim it and presume upon it does not make sense. Is she not kept fully busy with the question of whether the proclamation she is going to make, be it a great or a small opportunity, really *is* the good news of the Kingdom which it ought to be? Is she not fully occupied with unceasing prayer and work that her message may become ever more disciplined, more joyful, and more wholehearted, more thoroughly good news? Don't you think also that this good news, insofar as we are its effective spokesmen—though neither you nor I should too glibly assume that this is so—has in itself enough power to create new "spheres" and "opportunities" where the old ones may shrink more and more? Can't it even be true that the oppressors may one day marvel, dumbfounded, at these new spheres and opportunities of the church? Do not waste time and effort to defend the past, but let us run the risk and see which light will shine longer, provided things on our side go right! I am not familiar with the "peace pastors" whose admonition as quoted by you sounds somewhat bombastic to me. Perhaps some of them are right in their intentions, or at least not wrong. Perhaps others among them are collaborationists. Here is my advice: Do not chart your course, either positively or negatively, according to the "peace pastors," but set your eyes, as I once recommended in the presence of the "German Christians," "straight toward Jerusalem!"

7. *Isn't a commendable rash venture, a wanton haste, a premature experimenting when the apparently "crumbling façade" of the church is allowed to collapse more quickly than the circumstances require? Or has the hour struck for an extensive reconstruction of the church? Is there any criterion enabling us approximately to evaluate the momentous decisiveness of the hour?*

Answer: The hour for the extensive reconstruction of the church cannot have struck for you, surely, as long as you can still ask—in a rather academic way— for a criterion. And who knows whether the demolishing and rebuilding of the church will ever be the matter of a single decisive hour? It could take place —and in the history of all human potentialities and achievements this seems to be the rule—in a slow sequence, stretching over decades, of liberations from old and hitherto powerful strictures, and of commanding opportunities for new ventures. In your place I would anticipate some such isolated moments which are not arbitrarily judged "momentously decisive," but hold out the necessity and the freedom for immediate and concrete decisions. I would "watch out," and hold myself ready for these unequivocally permitted and commanded ventures. This would certainly not be possible without prayer. I would, therefore, look out not for what the circumstances may seem to require, but for the divine guidance which may be expected in any kind of circumstances. There could then be no talk of "rash venture, wanton haste, or premature experimenting." What is to be done may be and must be done with the decisiveness of wisdom, because it is done on the basis of guidance that is awaited and prayed for. I should like, without any intention of pressing or oppressing you, to point out that the Christian Church, as far as I can see, has at all times been well-disposed toward sweeping, if possible "eschatological," meditations and reflections, but frequently very reluctant indeed courageously to engage in specific and concrete ventures, because she has been lethargic and afraid. She has let pass many of those moments in which not everything but at least something could and ought to have been accomplished. Could it not be that you in the East Zone have been commissioned to lead the way for us also in that demolition and rebuilding of the church of which we spoke, not with great spectacular strides, but with small and therefore assured steps? I merely ask, but I do ask.

8. Pastors who are fugitives from the East German Republic are as a rule dismissed from their offices. Does not this employment of legal authority contradict the essence of the church who has a supreme op-

portunity for witness as she sets herself apart from the state in the employment of methods? Is the use of corrective power in this instance a legitimate way of exercising church discipline?

Answer: For a pastor to be a "fugitive" practically always means that he has abandoned his congregation at his own discretion, since his people are unable to follow him. There may be instances where we can humanly understand and forgive this. But even then the action is tantamount to the pastor's deposing himself from his office. What does the use of "corrective power" on the part of church authorities mean in this case except the confirmation of the fact that the pastor has cut himself off from the ministry in his congregation and from the church in which he served? It is quite true that the church has supreme opportunity for witness when she sets herself apart from the state in the choice of methods. But I cannot understand why the church should refrain from officially recognizing gently yet firmly the *fait accompli* which was not of her own choosing. When a pastor leaves the East German Republic, when he leaves for that matter his congregation, whatever his reasons may be, he cannot possibly claim before God or before men to possess the marks of a pastor and the rights that go with his office. Whether both of these can elsewhere be restored to him on the grounds of practical considerations is a question in itself on which I do not care to comment. A recollection: The Roman Catholic dean of the Cathedral of Cologne, a friend of mine, once told me how in the spring of 1945, as the Americans approached, he strictly forbade the clergy in his see to join the flight of their charges toward the East which was gaining momentum, and how he headed the clergy in solemn procession to meet the enemy. Another recollection: We had in Basle until recently a sizable group of East German theological students who worked with me very diligently and intelligently and used their time in the "West" in every respect sensibly and responsibly. I keep hoping that the barrier which was lowered at that time may again be lifted some day, especially as far as Basle is concerned! Do you know how it was when these young people took their leave from us? They assured me, emphatically if I remember correctly, without exception and on their own initiative, that they gladly returned to the East Zone because they knew that their place and their task were there. It may be that there are all kinds of special circumstances and conditions in your situation which I know nothing about and therefore cannot evaluate and appreciate. For the time being I must confess that what happened that time in Cologne and this undespairing return of my students to the East Zone seem better to me, both from a Christian and from a specifically theological standpoint, than the emigration of some evangelical pastors which you mention. I am therefore in no position to criticize the conduct of your church authorities in this matter.

*   *   *   *

I am at the end. But before I close, let me leave with you a good word in favor of the West German brethren at whose insufficient understanding of your situation and problems you have hinted with gentle resentment. It may indeed be that the brethren in the West have too little operative concern for you and for what is going on in your part of the country. But you see, that could have a close connection with what I tried to say at the beginning, in reference to 1 Peter 5:9. The West German brethren have been engaged now for years in a strenuous hand-to-hand fight with the powers and principalities, the spirits and demons in the land of the "economic miracle," with its thoughtless participation in NATO, with its remilitarization, its military chaplaincy contract, its preparation for atomic armament, its panicky fear of Russia, its crusading moods, its old Nazis, with all the disagreeable connotation the terms "Bonn" and "CDU" have there, both contentwise and personally, also for the Protestant churches. It ought not to be so, but I am afraid it is so: they simply lack the strength in this tribulation to take a more vital interest in your life and work. Be lenient with them, because they in their own situation must withstand an "adversary," though in an entirely different disguise, as well as they can, and must prove their solidarity with you in doing it. You may be assured that they cannot simply forget you, and you must trust them even when you have the feeling that they do not bear their due share of the burden. See to it, then, that you on your part do not forget the West German brethren in their battle, truly not an easy one either!

Where do I write all this? In a little farmhouse on a lonely height in the Bernese Emmenthal. I certainly wish I could give you a quick glance at the meadows, forests, and fields, the hills and snow-covered mountains that stretch before my eyes when I look up. All this is geographically and otherwise a long way from the cities, villages, and fields in the Mark, in Pomerania, in Oderbruch, in Thuringia, in Saxony, and other regions where you and your fellow pastors must work, "resist," and suffer! You must make allowance for this great distance and pardon me if you have the impression that here and there I have aimed and hit off the mark.

It would be a quite different matter if you had the feeling that I have here and there, and perhaps on the whole, smashed through doors that were already open or said things which you already know, perhaps even better than I do. Not only would this not vex me; it would make me very happy. Don't we read in Paul's letters (with which I don't want to have this letter compared!) in more than one place, *"You know, dear brethren . . ."*? What can one Christian say to other Christians that they do not in principle and perhaps also in fact know better than he? We owe it to each other, however, to remind one another of what we know and to repeat it again and again.

Whether this letter will reach you or not is a question in itself. If only your strict overlords will have the grace and the insight to let it get through to you and to others to whom it might be helpful! For my part I had you constantly in my thoughts while I have been writing. I think, though, that the letter will reach you in one way or another, even if I do not, as it had to be done with one of my letters to Holland during the war, microfilm and dispatch it in the hollow tooth of a special messenger.

So, for today, good-by. God, truly God, be with you! "Pray for us; we are doing the same for you!"

Yours,

KARL BARTH

End of August, 1958

AN ANSWER TO KARL BARTH
FROM EAST GERMANY

by Johannes Hamel

Dear Professor Barth:

Last October you wrote a letter to us pastors in East Germany. Meanwhile you have heard the various reactions in the newspapers of Switzerland and West Germany; even our own press in East Germany dealt with your letter, although the quotations were one-sided and the interpretation was misleading. While in the West you are now counted among the Communist fellow travelers, your letter gave equal offense to the East. It proved indeed too risky to quote it in its proper context, let alone to make it freely available for sale. Once again you seem to have chosen to sit on the fence, and, like a lonely bird on the rooftop, to sing a song that the roaring lions in the East and in the West cannot hear. How could they hear it!

I should like to express a hearty word of thanks to you, our fatherly teacher and friend. I have talked to many of my colleagues in the pastorate and in teaching. You have comforted, strengthened, and exhorted us by your letter, yet also warned us of this

and that abyss, that we may rightly fight the good
fight of the faith and hold fast unto him who has
won victory. I was therefore tremendously pleased
when the Bishop of one of our great *Landeskirchen*
in his Christmas letter encouraged all the pastors
under his care to suggest to their friends and rela-
tives in West Germany that they send your letter as
an appropriate gift under the Christmas tree.

All of us who received your letter are engaged in
a difficult struggle for the freedom of the gospel on
two fronts: against our own evil, lazy, and loveless
heart; and against a massive outside attack on faith,
witness, and obedience. With earnestness, urgency,
and relaxed humor you invite us in this inward and
outward struggle to hold fast unto the Lord who has
loved the godless people we are, and has embraced
in his love the world also.

At one point you are terribly concrete: what pastor
indeed could leave his congregation entrusted to him
in the East, self-confidently asserting his claim to a
pastoral office in the West! Truly, signs and miracles
happen. No other than Bishop Dibelius agrees with
you here. The comments on your letter in *Christ und
Welt* and in the *Sonntagsblatt* (though more moder-
ate) are simply foolish and far from reality. They
betray that German stubbornness which Swiss newspapers would not honor. If only your fellow citizens
realized how, since the beginning of your career and
now again, you have wrestled with this self-centered,
thwarted, and unteachable "German soul"!

Best of all, your letter gives us courage to read the Bible, to preach, to bear witness, and to make free decisions. The unhindered proclamation of the gospel in the Marxist world and the joyful obedience amidst a world that likes to display atheism—certainly a painstaking and risky task, desperate and driving to despair—are strengthened and affirmed in your letter.

Why should we argue with you that the concrete situations we have to face have some aspects that you in Basle are not in a position to know at the present time? You make this very reservation yourself in your letter. The writers in *Christ und Welt* and in the *Sonntagsblatt,* on the contrary, betray such a basic distance from the way and the misery, the joy, and the suffering of a pastor in "God's beloved East Zone" that they disqualify themselves from addressing a word of help and counsel to us.

May I conclude with the expression of my hope and joyful anticipation of the next volume of *Church Dogmatics,* asking you to continue to accept your joyous plight, undismayed by good and bad rumors, even to our benefit.

In heartfelt gratitude and in the name of many,
Naumburg

JOHANNES HAMEL

THE PROCLAMATION OF THE GOSPEL IN THE MARXIST WORLD

by Johannes Hamel

In this paper I shall limit myself to a consideration of that part of Central Europe which is dominated by Marxism. I thereby exclude the USSR and China. Although the countries of Central Europe have much in common historically, culturally, economically, politically, and ecclesiastically, they also have great differences. We only have to remember, e.g., the quite different political situations in Czechoslovakia, Hungary, Poland, and the DDR (German Democratic Republic). Similarly, the history and the present situation of the Christian churches in these countries are so diverse that the task of Christian witness may markedly differ from one country to another. A closer look at the Marxist world reveals that it has no uniformity. The churches there face situations, needs, possibilities, and tasks of such a different nature that we must strongly warn against an oversimplification of the problem of which Christian literature is very often guilty. The term "Marxist world" can be used only to describe a number of areas collectively where a party is in power which bases its ideology mainly on Marx, Engels, and Lenin. Any other use of the term is erroneous and dangerous.

Here we must face another preliminary question: Can the states dominated by Marxist parties be adequately conceived of as total or totalitarian, at least under certain aspects? It is well known that in the so-called free world this term is used to describe the political structures of Fascism (National Socialism) as well as of Marxism-Leninism. But is this equation correct? The use of the terms "free" and "totalitarian" may be understandable in a phenomenological description, e.g., of the difference between political and social life in Switzerland and Czechoslovakia. But as soon as we raise the question of the proclamation of the gospel, the widespread use of these terms becomes questionable.

Actually, the terms "free" and "totalitarian" merely refer to a number of concrete facts different from place to place and which have been expressed in a variety of ways among European societies and states in the more distant as well as in the more recent past!

The fundamental question is this: Does the Christian Church in the Marxist world hear and acknowledge her own gospel in its sovereignty and in all its dimensions? If so, she will receive and accept the Marxist world with its hard realities in the light of the gospel, and she will truly recognize her own situ-

ation and undertake her task in this world. Or does
the Christian Church understand the powers which
rule over her on the basis of a stereotype of ecclesiastical, political, social, and cultural traditions? If so, she
will neither recognize her own situation nor her own
task. Does the Christian Church deny the total sovereignty of the gospel of God over everything in
heaven and on earth? If so, she actually grants to the
Marxist world to declare and to understand itself as
atheistic and to behave accordingly. Or does the Christian Church proclaim publicly and privately, in small
and great things, that all powers and principalities
are already overcome and imprisoned through the res-
urrection of Jesus Christ? If so, she will reveal the
nature of atheism as a forlorn attempt to escape from
the reality of the Lord and Creator, or as a kind of
forlorn opposition against this reality. In popular
thought, e.g., in the books by Arthur Koestler, "Bolshevism" assumes the role of hell, filled by evil spirits.
Apart from objections to factual observations, we
should ask whether or not such a view betrays a latent
atheism as soon as it is expressed. The self-under-
standing of Marxism in its atheistic aspect is accepted by the Christian interpreter before he ever
has asked himself how Marxism is to be understood
in the light of the truth which he as a Christian has
to proclaim, and how it is to be encountered according to the gospel. At this point we must ask whether
or not the Christian Church in the Marxist world ex-
cludes from God's creation and providence one part

of the world, all of which is the designated realm for the proclamation of the gospel until the time of final judgment and redemption. Does the church want to interpret Marxism on her own strength alone, influenced not only by the gospel but also by other voices? Such an answer to Marxism will re-enforce its atheistic nature and merely vitalize it. The question has to be reversed. It is not: Is Marxist atheism a threat to the proclamation of the church? The question is: Could the failure on the part of the church to accept the proclamation in its divine power not help to spread atheism?

The many accounts of the life of the church in the East remind us of reports about flood disasters. The waters sweep over the fertile fields and the peaceful villages, devastating and destroying everything. Only a few hills and houses remain spared for the moment, but for how long? How long will the courage of the inhabitants last to resist the deadly flood? A view of Marxism analogous to a flood disaster is barred from hearing the voice of the gospel. Once we have visions of evil spirits we must not be surprised to find that our fear swallows up the fear of God and the trust in him. An analysis of Marxism in the same atheistic categories in which it defines itself proclaims the lie of a powerful, rival god. The answer to this fundamental question will determine whether or not the Christian Church will remain on the scene or be extinct, the words concerning the gates of hell or those concerning the salt which has lost its savor will be fulfilled, she will be silent and die or will live and proclaim the deeds of her Lord.

What does it mean to accept the Marxist world in the light of the gospel? In the history of the people of God we very often find a situation where Israel is faced with the question of who and what had come upon it and what should be the right response to the new order, the new lords who neither know nor proclaim the true God. During the second part of the eighth century the great power of Assyria conquered the area of Palestine. Nations were uprooted and deported, customs and laws were changed, gods were introduced as symbols of the new rule. The reaction of the people, their king, their priests, and their aristocracy was quite natural: a foreign power which worships idols has attacked the chosen people. They believed that they had to resist, as long as courage lasted, this invasion of evil in the name of the Lord; but if it were apparent that they were mistaken, that the foreign gods were stronger, they could then but surrender to their superior strength, reluctantly and facing the consequences. Israel's attitude ranged from illusion about the seriousness of the situation to constant attempts to line up Egypt's power on its side and to play this as a trump card; it ranged from ecstasy about partial successes to deep despair, irrational "metaphysical" anxiety, and basic doubts about God's gracious election. Chapters 1–39 of Isaiah provide colorful illustrations of such actions and reactions.

This drama is repeated inside and outside Jerusalem during the last third of the seventh century and the first third of the sixth century, now even more clearly recognizable and more sharply drawn. Assyria's power declines and Babylon rises. The king, the aristocracy, the nation, and the priesthood react in unison to the new situation, its new possibilities, threats, hopes, and tasks. They are supported by the "prophets," not a new but now a much more influential group. "This is the temple of the Lord" (Jeremiah 7:4) is the uniting slogan. It is the basis of resistance, the source of inspiration for the defense of country and religion. God has no choice but to protect the people which call on him. This conviction determines also the attitude toward such a nonconformist as Jeremiah. He is all the more suspect as a defeatist, because the growing power of Babylon naturally attracts collaborators who cast their lot with the rising star out of pragmatic motives (there are even refugees in the camp of Nebuchadnezzar!). What else could Jeremiah be but a weakling and a traitor? The people had just dared an ecclesiastical reformation under Josiah, doing away with the Assyrian idols. Was it not a renewed church, confessing its Lord and putting away what was foul and old? Now her existence is threatened from the outside. When Nebuchadnezzar enters Jerusalem for the first time and deports its elite to the Euphrates, this group continues to be comforted by the prophetic proclamation that they just had to hibernate for a short time in the land of the foreign gods. Their God would soon restore the old order. In fact, he had no other choice (cf. Jeremiah 29)!

The middle of the sixth century witnesses the breath-taking rise of Persia as a world power. Babylon's empire begins to break up. Resignation among the Jewish exiles turns into horror. They had barely managed to preserve the ancient faith in their synagogues, they had hibernated, and now the new power threatens to trample it all down. The waters of this storm are closing in on the frail boat of Israel. Is any other reaction possible? Is there any hope left for this people? Is their faith not antiquated, bound to be wiped out by the powers and ideologies which are shaping the future?

Further, let us point to a historical development during the last half of the first century A.D. and extending into the first decades of the second. Early Christianity emerges first as a Jewish sect and is thereby considered a *"religio licita."* Its Lord has been sentenced and executed by a Roman governor, and it faces some Jewish antagonism. But during these first years its existence is barely noticed. The situation changes gradually, partly because of missionary activity, partly because of the intensified opposition of Judaism against these apostates. Finally, the Jewish insurgence, leading at the outset to the Jewish war of 68–70 A.D., faces the church with the problem of how to live under idolatrous emperors, authorities, and laws while confessing Christ as Lord

over the world. There seemed to be no third alternative between militant zealotism and a gnostic dep-
recation of all external realities, between revolt and
an attitude of external submission to the emperor
while inwardly despising him.

In these periods of history the people of God had
to face the question as to whether or not the indi-
cated reactions, real or possible, to submission under
Assyria, Babylonia, Persia, and the Roman emperor
represented the final word of wisdom. Was their
action always to be dictated by either revolt or alignment? The preaching of Isaiah, Jeremiah, the unknown preacher in the middle of the sixth century
(Isaiah 40–55), and the summaries of the early
church's proclamation in various parts of the New
Testament, all deny this either/or alternative.
Neither do they propagate a middle line between
the two extremes. (This was the attitude of the Phari-
saic party up to the Jewish war!)

The prophets reach down to a deeper level and
proclaim these bearers of new power and order to be
the instruments of Israel's Lord who created the uni-
verse. In the encounter with Assyria, Babylonia, the
Persian ruler, and the emperor, the people of God
meet the Lord himself. This is the good news, unani-
mously proclaimed by prophets and apostles. This
news has always been terrifying to God's people. It is
illustrated by the changes in the text, made by the
Septuagint at several points in Isaiah, Jeremiah, and
Deutero-Isaiah. Apparently, the Jewish community

felt that it was too radical to proclaim Assyria as the "rod of anger," "the staff of my fury." "Against a godless nation I send him, and against the people of my wrath I command him. . . . But he does not so intend, and his mind does not so think" (Isaiah 10:5 ff.). Similarly, it was difficult to accept Jeremiah's assertion that Nebuchadnezzar, of all people, should be the servant of God (25:9): "It is I who by my great power and my outstretched arm have made the earth, with the men and animals that are on the earth, and I give it to whomever it seems right to me. Now I have given all these lands into the hand of Nebuchadnezzar, the king of Babylon, my servant, and I have given him also the beasts of the field to serve him. All the nations shall serve him and his son and his grandson. . . . So do not listen to your prophets, your diviners, your dreamers, your soothsayers, your sorcerers, who are saying to you: 'You shall not serve the king of Babylon' " (27:5 ff.). Omission and revision were likewise used by the translators of the Bible into Greek, to resist the message which proclaimed the pagan Cyrus as the Messiah of the Lord!

Paul continues substantially in the vein of the prophets when he calls the Roman authorities, even the tax collectors, "God's servants" (Romans 13:1 ff.). The same good news is proclaimed in the following decades and is found in the pastoral epistles, in 1 Peter, and in Revelation. In Revelation 13 the church which suffers under the anti-Christian power of the beast receives the following word of comfort:

the beast is allowed to exercise authority (vss. 5, 7, 15) for a short while, namely, forty-two months (vs. 5). But the church which is defenseless in the hands of the beast is exhorted in verse 10 to have the faith and endurance of the saints. They are actually in the hand of the Holy One who has determined the limits of the beast's power. Even in the face of imprisonment and death the church can continue on the good path which is protected by God. "If anyone is to be taken captive, to captivity he goes; if anyone is slain with the sword, with the sword must he be slain" (according to the ancient, correct version). The church does not end up in hell, but always remains under the victorious power of the Lamb who has conquered. She follows her Lord not only in spite of her defenseless suffering, but in it.

The Passion stories, too, present this same good news: Priests and Pontius Pilate are believed to be instruments of God's mercy and compassion as he deals with the world. Matthew precedes his report about the decision of the high priests, scribes, and elders with the following saying of Jesus: "You know that after two days the Passover is coming, and the Son of man will be delivered up to be crucified." The Jewish authorities are proclaimed and accepted as the executors of God's plan of salvation (cf. Matthew 26:1 ff.). In John's Gospel Jesus confesses in front of Pilate that he is, in fact, a king, that his kingdom is not of this world. It is as high above every other

kingdom as the creator is above the creatures. He
further asserts that the Roman governor had no
power over him "unless it had been given you from
above" (John 18:36 f. and 19:11). Finally, we should
remember the message of Acts with its supposedly
friendly tendency toward the state. The author in
his many accounts reaffirms the original gospel. God
uses the Roman authorities in his service, without
their being aware of it. Here the history of the early
church becomes a testimony to an unbounding trust,
grounded in the revealed act of the God and Father
of Jesus Christ who has placed the ruling powers
within their limits and in his service. The author,
writing during the last years of the first century, does
exhibit a certain apologetic tendency, but, in substance, he repeats, although in his own colorful and
legendary style, the earlier proclamation.

The proclamation of the gospel makes the foreign
powers and their rule a part of God's created world.
But it does not limit itself to calling these men and
these powers servants of God for the benefit of God's
people. From Isaiah to the New Testament this message is also the announcement of the judge. He comes
to judge his people who refuse to obey their Lord.
Assyria is truly the rod of anger; Nebuchadnezzar is
sent out "because you do not pay heed to my word."
Through Cyrus, the Lord puts to shame the despair
and unbelief of his people. The Roman authorities
"do not bear the sword in vain; they are the servants
of God to execute his wrath on the wrongdoer." Paul

addresses this as a warning to the Christians in Rome!
Similarly, 1 Peter (2:11) repeats the warning, putting
it even more sharply. In the event that the church
receives blows at the hands of the rulers, she shall
"let none of you suffer as a murderer, or a thief, or
a wrongdoer, or a mischief-maker; yet if one suffers
as a Christian, let him not be ashamed, but under
that name let him glorify God. For the time has come
for the judgment to begin with the household of
God" (4:15 ff.). It is God's will not eternally to condemn but eternally to save his people. Therefore, he
calls them to repentance in the encounter with the
ruling powers. The call to endure arises out of the
call to return to the Lord who searches in vain for
the faithfulness of his people. The synagogue rejects
the call to repentance, issued by John the Baptist and
his Christ. Therefore, it is finally trapped in the
revolt against the foreign Roman power in the name
of the God of Israel. The Christian Church can escape the Scylla of revolt and the Charybdis of alignment and denial only when she bows to the call of
God's repentance, upon whom depend also the rulers
who might afflict her. The bitterness about the emperor, real or possible, is challenged by the proclamation to face God's judgment which extends to all
powers.

A further element of this proclamation needs to be
underscored. The people need constantly to know
that the rule of an idolatrous power may put an end
to their worship and their faith, and may destroy

them or at least endanger their existence. Nevertheless, the announcement of God's work through these
servants and executors of his judgment also contains
the promise of a new era of redemption for this
people and for all who live in this estranged world.
The various accounts of the promise of such a new
era are well known. I refer to Isaiah 4:9 and 11; the
proclamation of the new covenant in Jeremiah 31:33
ff.; Isaiah 40–55, in itself one long announcement of
redemption for the nations and for Israel; and, finally,
the passages in the New Testament about the emperor, his officials, and his judgments. They are always the persons to whom the gospel is addressed.
They provide the occasions for the Spirit to give the
word in due time. They proffer the great opportunities to let the word take its course.

Again, Acts contains numerous illustrations of such
a proclamation. The investigation by the Sanhedrin
of the activity of Peter and John is the occasion of
a confession wrought by the Spirit (4:1 ff.) and a
prayer of the community, inspired by the Spirit
(4:23 ff.; cf. also 5:17 ff.). The accusation of Stephen
causes his powerful testimony which pierces the souls
of his executioners, and in his intercession for them
he enters true discipleship (6:8–7:59). Saul destroys
the church wherever he can, and many have to flee:
"Now those who were scattered went about preaching
the word" (8:4, 11:19). Saul's raging opposition to
the church, with its horrors of torture and murder
(cf. his strongest description in 26:9 ff.), is only the

short prelude of darkness to the light of Damascus
and the long years of his apostolate. His imprisonment in Jerusalem is interpreted as opening the way
for his testimony in Rome and before the emperor
(23:11, 27:23). In his letter to the Philippians he answers the anxious question of the church in Philippi
concerning his imprisonment with the following
words: "I want you to know, brethren, that what has
happened to me has really served to advance the gospel, so that it has become known throughout the
whole practorian guard and to all the rest that my
imprisonment is for Christ; and most of the brethren
have been made confident in the Lord because of
my imprisonment, and are much more bold to speak
the word of God without fear" (Philippians 1:12 ff.).
God has prepared the precious gift of the spread of
his Word for the repentant church which believes in
the power of the gospel over the world's rulers.

A fourth insight is given to the church with this
proclamation. She may hear, believe, and experience
that the Lord ever again makes room for his people
to live. He does it miraculously through these same
servants and executors, and he does it contrary to all
expectations. In the midst of persecutions he makes it
possible to do good, to preserve justice, to maintain
a greater or lesser degree of human freedom, and to
be active in public affairs. Jeremiah's letter (29:1 ff.)
to the deported Jews in Babylonia is a good illustra-
tion. He encourages them to build houses, to plant
their vineyards, to found families, to seek the best for

their city (Babylon!) and to pray for it, "for in its welfare you will find your welfare." How is it possible
for Israel and Babel to make common cause, as is
suggested in this shocking letter? Jeremiah proclaims
the God who in his goodness and mercy is also the
God of Babel. In the midst of idolatry, no less ramp-
ant in Babel than it is today, God creates opportunities for his people to coexist with those blind Baby-
lonians, while paganism surrounds them. The pious
protested strongly this strange prophecy of coexistence. They denounced the strange prophet by letter
before the ecclesiastical authorities in Jerusalem, with
the friendly suggestion to put him in jail and on
the block.

But the pious of all times argue quite logically
from the reality of idolatry and its imperialistic ideology. They conclude that the existence of the Church
of God is made impossible because every aspect of
life is exposed to the claims of this idolatry. They
start out with the recognition of the terrible reality
of idolatry and end up with an imaginary God and
an illusionary existence. Their life at times assumes
the form of zealotism, bent on extinguishing the godless. But the proclamation of the gospel indicates the
room for daily prayer, daily faith and action—and
suffering. The pious mass wants to erect a theocracy,
but the gospel tells us of God's merciful lordship even
over Babylon. The zealots build the kingdom of God,
but they destroy human possibilities of action. The
gospel allows us to count on God's power only and

grants us human action through its miraculous power.

Now we can understand the positive attitude of the New Testament passages, already mentioned, which describe the responsibilities and actions of the governments and the contributions of the church for the good of the order. They are exhortations to have faith, to be obedient, to pray. They bespeak the truth that God will employ the governments in spite of their idolatry, that the life and actions of Christians are possible and meaningful in regard to and under the guidance of these governments. Time and again God creates loopholes, so to speak, open space in the midst of closed systems of unbelief and hatred of God. Here the possibility is offered and realized for doing the good, reasonable, and well-pleasing, although these systems theoretically seem to leave no room for such action. Only hell itself can prevent us from rendering praise and obedience to God. But here on earth the church will not be overcome by the gates of hell as long as she holds fast to confessing his name.

*   *   *

We shall now return from biblical considerations to the question of proclaiming the gospel in the Marxist world. We shall attempt to remain faithful to the biblical insights. This means, first of all, that we have to free ourselves from the reaction of the predominant Christian middle class to the political power structures of Marxism-Leninism. We do not need to describe this reaction any more. It is only too well known and too popular. Also, it matters little whether or not it is advanced from the side of Roman Catholicism, liberalism, or official Protestantism. The same mistake is common to all three views, and it is often illustrated in sermons. First, the power of sin is presented in colorful and concrete terms. This is supposed to furnish the background for divine forgiveness, but the latter is never quite convincing. On both sides of the Iron Curtain the fundamental assumption that "Bolshevism" spells the end of freedom, of humanitarianism, of culture and Christendom, is unquestioned. The history of the last forty years is supposed to prove beyond doubt that Bolshevism is a basically anti-Christian phenomenon, to be opposed, if necessary, with arms in order to give back to the nations under its rule the possibility of living a Christian life. We are told that the totalitarian state by definition leaves no choice for the people under it but to conform, outwardly and increasingly inwardly. Arguments to the contrary are refuted with a list of quotations from Communist literature and Communist newspapers.

However, there are also quite a few Christians and theologians in the churches in the East who argue on the other side. They, too, are backed up by undeniable facts and statements which seem to prove the contrary. They rightly point to the life of the Orthodox Church in the USSR which, according to recent observations, has experienced a remarkable growth during the last fifteen years. They remind us of the continuing financial support and special contributions which the government grants to the churches. Churches are full in Czechoslovakia, Hungary, and Poland. The DDR spends enormous sums every year for the six theological faculties, including large grants for scholarships. The churches enjoy an extraordinary amount of freedom in comparison with the situation under the Hitler regime. Also, we must not forget that the churches in the DDR are granted a number of privileges which are denied to other organizations. It is an undeniable fact that since 1945 elections, in the DDR especially, of synod representatives and general church officers, as well as appointments of ministers, proceed more freely and with less influence from the outside than has ever been the case in the history of these churches. Nobody is prevented from attending worship services. The violation of the Sabbath by a number of companies is also the practice in the West German steel industry and has just recently been introduced elsewhere over the protest of the ecclesiastical authorities.

We could continue this list of facts and none of them could be contested. Furthermore, a quite different view of the social structure of Marxism-Leninism from that of the Christian middle class reaction is often connected with these indications. This testifies in manifold ways to the life of the church in these countries. I merely recall for you the replies by Dr. Hromadka to the critics of the Marxist world, wherein he reveals the impasses and the dark spots of the "Western" world which he knows from his own experience over many years. It is not necessary to point to the new life emerging in China, or developments in the USSR—we have excluded them from our considerations. It is sufficient to have a look at the socialist accomplishments of the Peoples' Democracies, at least partially acknowledged by the Social Democratic parties of the West. Details are well known in this area.

We seem to be caught in diametrically opposed views and reactions with regard to the Marxist world. Both are based on facts, so that neither can ever completely refute the other. We shall escape this dilemma only if we are prepared to accept this world anew on the basis of the preaching of the prophets and apostles. We must desist once and for all from placing Christianity and its teaching into the strait jacket of Christian anti-communism or pro-communism. A process of rethinking is needed that will not allow either side to retain its present position. Christian witness must count on the fact that the good news of God has something new to say to us. In the face of the Marxist world this news cannot be used by us for any of our purposes. It will not elicit the consent or applause of the masses and the rulers on either side, unless they let themselves be called to repentance by the Spirit. It is not a matter of the "interpretation" of history. Interpretation is always an attempt to insert a new fact into already existing patterns of history in order to explain it and to gain control over it. But the gospel does not interpret history, it makes history. Furthermore, it announces this history and thereby it opens the narrow way for us whereon we can follow our Lord.

The issue is, first of all: whether the Christian Church in the Marxist world openly confesses that her own Lord and Master meets her in the encounter with these powers and structures. He has taken the Marxists into his service, he has used them as his instruments and is still using them. To suppress this truth means for the church to deny her faith. Whatever may have to be said about Marxism, it is certain that in the encounter with it we do not enter godless territory or a no man's land outside the reach of the gospel. This is not a province where God's word is neutral, an inferno from which God should save us if he can. On the contrary, as messengers of Jesus Christ we proclaim that through the rise of the Marxist world God has opened for us a new page of his history which began with Easter and ends with the Second Coming. In the face of these powers God calls his people, treading the path of the cross, to new obedience, new praise, new prayer, new endurance. He calls for the renewal of our church and for the transformation of her patterns in order that she may serve him in greater faithfulness. If we hear the gospel today, we shall not be concerned with our defense against the numerous and frightful attacks on church, Christendom, and godliness. Before ever we define our attitude with regard to these attacks, we shall have to face God's salutary attack on his people by means of these men and these powers. He smites us in mercy, and the means he chooses are wholly secondary. He does not abandon us to our evil intentions which draw condemnation upon us. He throws us into such a whirl that we risk losing our wits. He drives us out of our foul and rotten ecclesiastical palaces of past centuries and forces us through his "servants" to become strangers and pilgrims, wandering to meet their Lord. He comes to clean his house with an iron broom—and how much less important is the broom beside him who handles it?

The Marxists as servants of God! Who will believe it? Who will reckon with this fact? Who will listen to this kind of preaching? It is not a justification of the Marxists, least of all a sublimation of their thinking, their statements and actions. It is even less an abasement or degradation. For this role ascribes to them a tremendous dignity. It places them in direct relationship to the Kingdom. They stand over against the Christian Church by virtue of a divine directive, and the church must honor their service by giving God the honor with fear and trembling. The gospel places us right next to these men. It exposes us to their power. But we would pass God by in our prayers and our actions if we were to refuse to have anything to do with them.

Here we must guard against a misunderstanding. We are dealing with messengers and servants of God, with his ax and his rod, his staff and the instrument of his power over us. But these structures in themselves are not a disclosure of the Father of Jesus Christ, not a divine revelation, not God's gracious and merciful word, not "God's secular word" to us. The ax could also be swung by Satan's hand. The rod could kill instead of chastising us for our salvation. The instrument could also be used for destruction. His Word proclaims, however, that it is he who uses it in order to save us, his people, from the misery of our sins. This same Word proclaims him as the Lord over these servants. "Shall the ax vaunt itself over him who hews with it, or the saw magnify itself against him who wields it? As if a rod should wield him who lifts it, or as if a staff should lift him who is not wood!" (Isaiah 10:15). The Lord is free to call his servants and to dismiss them, to swing the ax and to lay it aside, to use the staff and to break it.

In the light of this proclamation it is immaterial whether we think that Marxism is good or bad. Either view is a denial of the gospel if it becomes our primary concern. The gospel opens up a dimension in which good and bad are no longer distributed along the lines defined by a basically atheistic view. This view is widespread even in the churches: one either anxiously opposes the attack of Marxism or one encourages it in the name of Christ. The gospel makes us free people who do not rebel against the visitation of God calling us to repentance by sending us these servants. The gospel releases us from bitter silence and from glorifying gossip. It looses our tongues for the praise of God whose majesty draws into his service even Marxism and the Marxists.

In recent discussions it has often been asked whether a Communist government (including Politbureau and Central Committee) could be considered as "authorities" in the sense of Romans 13. The question already implies that certain rules must be observed by the "authorities" before the church can honor them with this attribute. But regardless of approval or disapproval this approach fails to recognize that in Romans 13 the authorities are announced as a part of God's Word so that we may give glory to God. He uses them as his servants for our own good, although not necessarily to our own liking. The church has no reason to develop any theories about the nature of the state in general or of a particular state. Of course, it is possible to search the New Testament for a judgment concerning the state, but in so doing we shall bypass the central affirmation of the gospel in this area. We cannot place ourselves above the state and hand out judgments. Our place is below the powers and the rulers. We are in front of the seat of judgment from whence we receive our word of command and our judgment.

This is our situation, and it is the gospel, good news, that it is so. For the gospel liberates the people of God from the terrible isolation, and from the possibility of being left to themselves before the Marxist camp. For the church is constantly tempted to ask:

"Are we not completely at the mercy of this power? Does not our future depend on its favor or disfavor toward us? Has Marxist power perhaps won the day while God remains silent?" Have we not all heard this voice of temptation during the last years, in our own heart as well as from others? Have we not all had occasion to observe how, here and there, few or many yielded to it? They immediately had to face the terrible consequence which presented itself to them under two forms, because the one cannot exist without the other. There are those in the church who rise to a positive appreciation of Marxism. They discover a philosophy of history which recognizes in Marxism the new era for the good of humanity. It sways the future while the "West" stumbles toward its grave. But others rise against them. In angry indignation they attack everything which is incompatible with the conception of a law-abiding state. For them it is of the essence of Christian faith to oppose Marxism and to condemn it as immoral and irreligious.

Both sides have substituted faith for a world-view, judgment for listening, a self-styled position for obedience. No wonder that the boat of the church is aimlessly drifting, while her members hearken to this voice of temptation. The political powers in East and West will play their tricks on the church, and she will inevitably break apart into hostile parties because she refuses to be held together by a common listening to the Word. Behind the ecclesiastical adversaries the shadows or even the bodies of the politicians already

emerge, talking about the present cold war and pointing to the threat of a future hot war. A terrible mael-
strom transforms the messengers of the sovereign
Lord in religious communities, so that each follows
the decisions, proclamations, and actions of the politicians and places upon them their religious, theological, or Christian "stamp." Nobody dares to spell
out the conclusions, although they are obvious: It is
possible for a Christian to allow or even to demand
"world revolution" in the case of the East, or the
battle for "freedom" and "liberation" in the case of
the West, and to permit the use of nuclear weapons
for the pursuit of either goal. In the end there would
be military chaplains on either side of the front line
with much to say but nothing to proclaim. Both sides
express unbelief. The fear of further spread of communism dictates to the church the task of producing
the ethical and philosophical attitude required for
resistance, for the production of arms, and possibly
for their use. On the other side, the fascination of
Christians by the Marxist world, its manifold prog-
ress, its impressive successes, and especially its fastly
growing power, leads to mental and spiritual surrender to this imposing reality. It leads to a Christian
party line about the world revolutionary movement.

At the time of Jeremiah, Israel was split into an
Egyptian and a Babylonian party. Rescue was expected either from the North or from the South. The
prophet urged the people to break away from its
dreams and aspirations. He called for repentance

which would recognize and acknowledge the hard-headed Babylonian ruler as the servant of the true Israel. No simple "third way" is possible in the face of the Marxist world and its counterpart either. However, we are to listen to the proclamation concerning the Lord over the world who knows how to use the Marxist regime as an instrument of his gracious will. Having carefully listened to it, we shall go on to find the narrow path where peacemakers can perform their rescue service, where God is feared above all things, where the rulers are honored, and where eternal salvation is assured.

The encounter with the Marxist world raises a further question for the church. Is she prepared to accept God's judging and living Word as it breaks into her life in the form of these powers? In the rise of Marxism, the judge appears himself to settle accounts with his church, according to his severe mercy. He uses his servants to drive the accused before his throne. Are we preaching the Word of divine judgment over the life of our congregations and their members? Does his Word have free course among us, enabling us to examine our churches critically? Does our preaching break through the Marxist criticism to the divine criticism which is much more serious, more merciful, and more wholesome than the most pointed criticism of Marxism or our self-criticism? Again, we have to overcome the dilemma in which we are easily caught. It is the dilemma of either accepting the Marxist criticism of the church or of defending our-

selves against all attacks. Both alternatives are deadly
for the church, for they silence her as a voice for
the gospel.

It is only too easy to confuse the critical voice of
Marxism with God's voice, to identify the Marxist
policy regarding the church with God's action toward
his people. Are not the Christian religion and the
church groups residues of certain sociological classes,
identified with declining social structures? Is Christianity today more than a glorified *bourgeoisie*,
doomed to collapse? Isn't faith a preliminary substi-
tute for the emerging scientific knowledge? Isn't the
church an ideological front for the liberal-capitalistic
order of society? Isn't the church in Marxist territory
a "fifth column" of capitalism? Aren't her members
fellow travelers of the "West" against the "East"?
Isn't the church a last resort of liberal thought and
life? Isn't the residue of a Christian life, especially
infant baptism, confirmation of teen-agers, wedding,
funeral, church taxes, Christmas, Easter, Thanks-
giving, Christian education, etc., an expression not
of faith, but merely of pagan customs with Christian
coating, completely divorced from the rest of people's
life? The church's speaking and acting results in the
creation of a bad conscience in those who actually
have lost faith. The huge church buildings are empty;
large membership lists are merely a façade. The number of pastors and Christian educators is much too
large. These can only be maintained through state
support, the privilege of church taxation, and help

from the West. Is not this a colossus on feet of clay? A structure full of cracks to be torn down with a good conscience, especially if the operation is carefully planned and carried out with all deliberate speed? Isn't the sermon a dull presentation, irrelevant to modern life, delivered by paid functionaries without any deep conviction? Isn't the resistance on the part of the ecclesiastical leaders a result of political resentment? Hasn't the courage to make an open confession become such a rare sight that it rightly can be considered as the exception rather than the rule?

Nietzsche said: "What falls, might as well be pushed over." Is Marxism not right to engage in this business with its reputable energy, wisdom, endurance, patience, and craftiness? Is not its thesis very logical, according to which there will be some people for a longer or shorter time to come who will want to satisfy their religious needs, and that this will be made possible until their natural extinction? The church is to understand herself as the people of God. But can we see any sign of it? She calls herself the community of Jesus Christ. But where does she act accordingly? What else is there for Marxism to see but a passive audience, listening to sermons and looking at ceremonies, and the activities of paid ecclesiastical specialists?

In the light of this self-confident criticism and its increasing success it is not at all surprising that certain church circles seek to align themselves with this power. They are eager to participate in this great

movement at any price. They search for a spot in this
system where they will be tolerated or even wanted,
and where they can be welcomed and esteemed collaborators. It is quite understandable to find them
engaged in an effort to work out and prove a biblical
basis for common goals of Marxism and Christianity:
"The Humanization of the Social Order," the struggle for "peace," the elimination of "exploitation," the
battle against "imperialism" and "colonialism," the
realization of "justice on earth," the fight against
"warmongers," "Fascism," etc.! "A Christian says Yes
to Karl Marx!" Is this really so absurd as it might
sound? We cannot deny that these circles are deeply
sensitive to the corruption of the church as revealed
by Marxism, and that they are sincerely determined
to preserve and renew within the Marxist world
the imperishable religious and moral values of
Christianity.

Against this tide stands a countermovement inside
and outside the Marxist realm. While it admits the
faults and weaknesses of the existing church, it recognizes in the rise of Marxism nothing else but the
final attack of atheism and the antichrist and calls
for determined resistance. This is not the time for
fatal self-criticism which only weakens and confuses
the ranks! Now is the moment to close the ranks and
to stand firm! A call is issued by this countermovement for spiritual resistance, for steadfastness until
the arrival of a better day. Bible and tradition are
marshaled and we are referred to analogous develop-

ments in the history of the church. The "totalitarian state," the beast from the abyss, can only be met with a final No, regardless of whether it may have propagated and accomplished many positive and good things. Where the church is under its domination, she will have to suffer for her resistance. Where she is not yet overpowered by it, she has to call for spiritual, moral, political, and, if necessary, for military defense. Behind the Marxist attack and criticism nobody else but the ancient foe is at work, bent on wiping out all faith in God. And when the hour comes, the same will hold with regard to communism as with regard to Assyria of old: "We will speed upon horses!" (Isaiah 30:16). Evil is to be fought with every means, even with arms, if necessary.

Such a church, torn within herself, hungers for the call to repentance which places her before the divine judge and frees her from the two forms of bondage to Marxism. Only the proclamation of repentance can heal the hopeless and devastating divisions which today threaten the existence of church and humanity. God himself enters into judgment with us in the encounter with Marxism. He is the smelter who wants to separate pure from impure. He struggles for the renewal of the church, calling her from her longstanding sins in shame and remorse. We cannot confuse Marxism with God's judgment and appeal. Therefore, nothing is accomplished by seeking salvation for the church in the acceptance of its criticism and by participation in its movement. Whoever would save his life will lose it; this applies here too. Behind human accusations, God's accusation must be heard and acknowledged. Behind fanatic ideologies stands the Holy One, threatening to remove our lampstand from its place and to spew us out from his mouth. It is not sufficient to admit the weaknesses and sins of the existing church which "naturally she has, for all men are sinners." This is no basis for a call to defense. We shall fight with inept weapons and shall not endure in the spiritual battle which is, in fact, ours. We are not contending against flesh and blood, but against the evil spirits under heaven which cannot be limited to one form of human rebellion against God. Whoever limits evil is already in the grip of the evil one! Professor Hromadka has once stated that we do not need to fear a godless world, but rather a godless and unbelieving church.

What is at stake is our readiness, inwardly and outwardly, to proclaim and to believe the divine smelting as our salvation, not to escape it and to trust that God in his grace will raise us up through his judgment. As the church accepts this two-edged sword, she will be given the right weapons against all attacks of the evil foe on the right and on the left. By repenting and turning away from her trespasses, she will remain strong and will escape all temptations. The statement that a church could not survive under communism is just as much devoid of repentance as the counterstatement that life is possible given a few concessions or more thoroughgoing changes of her order and views. The church, even under Marxism, constantly lives from God's promise not to put an end to her life, but to renew her through his Word as it is accepted in repentance. If he calls us to turn around and if we hear his voice, we shall not refuse soberly and seriously to examine whether or not the uncomfortable questions of Marxism indicate that God calls for changes in our life. In many respects we shall be able to go along with its criticism, but Jesus Christ will transform even this criticism into his call for the renewal of the church. We live by the promise that the judge guards and protects us on this path of repentance. His marvelous intervention will keep us day by day from defending ourselves and from conforming to the friend-foe scheme of the Marxists. In his own person he presents our enemies to us as those whom we are to love. Then we shall realize, to our amazement, that "Christ did not die against Karl Marx, but for us all," as Dr. Heinemann stated during that memorable hour in the Bonn Parliament in January, 1958. In repentance we attain the freedom which leads us on the narrow path where we are free from being either fellow travelers of Marxism or its enemies. Only here the claim becomes valid that the church is not concerned about the preservation or recovery of the *status quo,* but solely about the continuing advance of the gospel in the midst of a crooked and perverted generation.

Does God continue to speak? This question, too, arises out of the Marxist claim that, according to

irrefutable laws, the bell tolls for the Christian
Church. Do we perhaps agree? Do we, at least secretly,
harbor some doubts: "Could it really be true? Are we
fighting for a lost cause? Does not the end of Christian civilization spell the end of the Christian faith?"
Who is not at times tired and dismayed? Who would
not like to give up sometimes? Who would not want
to join in the outburst of Elijah: "It is enough; now,
O Lord, take away my life; for I am no better than
my fathers" (1 Kings 19:4). Is the Western world not
attractive, with its possibilities for impressive ecclesiastical activities, where the Christian faith is protected and where privileges are granted to the church
and her members? Look at the Middle East and
North Africa, once the center of flowering church
life. Are not they a sign that present history might be
threatening to turn in that direction? Is it not true
that group after group in the Marxist world—and not
only there!—is seized by the resignation which Paul
calls the worldly grief, producing death?

Of course we could also point to some positive
signs, like the beginnings of a renewed missionary
effort in the church. But this does not provide any
firm ground on which to stand. These signs are like
friendly bonuses of our Lord, and they receive and
preserve their value only in connection with the main
gift. Some seek comfort in the speculation that a sud-
den turn of events could restore all the now closed
opportunities for the church's work. Objections to
this "comfort" are numerous. The spectacle, offered

by the churches which enjoy these greater opportunities, robs this "comfort" of its strength and truth. Although Christians in those churches are granted legal "protection" or even privileges for their way of life and their views, they are incapable of taking advantage of this much larger room for their activities in behalf of the gospel. As far as I can judge, the question of the acceptance of the gospel is no less pressing and justified than in the Marxist world. We need a quite different knowledge and promise of comfort.

Living within the Marxist world, can we understand the stories, Psalms, prophecies, parables, and letters of the Bible in any other way than as being directly addressed to the church in this world? In fact, God's Word has assumed a strange straightforwardness, whether it be in church school, the sermon, in group Bible study, or in personal conversation. The thick walls of nineteen hundred years have come down. Nothing stands between us and the biblical Word. The Bible speaks to our situation as never before. It seems as if the biblical characters have again become alive among us, drawing us to their side as actors in the divine drama, almost against our will. Many of us can testify of an instance when suddenly we find ourselves mirrored in Scriptures, and with us, the estranged, the indifferent, and the enemies. A case in point is the reaction of a group of young people when their religious instructor read to them the 24th chapter of the Gospel according to St. Matthew. It first caused breathless silence and then the

response: "It sounds as if this was written for us."
The aggressiveness of atheism is in itself a sign of the
threatening effect of the word "God" and therefore
of God's Word. "Affliction teaches us to understand
the Word." We know that Luther gave a wrong translation of this verse, because understanding is not a
natural consequence of affliction. Temptation can
also devour. But God's comfort and warning miraculously enter our lives when we read the Bible, when
we pray, preach, listen, and teach. He sends out his
Word to be thrown among the multitude. Many turn
toward it in opposition or with acceptance and take
notice of the witness of Christians. For believers it
has become strangely simple to turn their lives into
commentaries on the gospel. The question of how to
live as a Christian among non-Christians has been
surprisingly simplified, although it has lost nothing
of its gravity. The insight breaks through that the
field is white for the harvest and that God arises to
seek and to save what is lost. Unless we close our eyes,
we are bound to see with joy that God is announcing
a new day of evangelization. If we listen to the gospel,
we can hear only this and nothing else.

Nevertheless: Are we perhaps stubbornly and anxiously closing our ears to his Word? Are we deliber-
ately rejecting this great divine blessing? Do we prefer our unbelief and our flesh—and the fleshpots of
Egypt!—to the *viva vox evangelii?* Do we bypass
God's visitation in our own inexcusable hardness of
heart? Do we look back like Lot's wife did for her

burning house, only to become a pillar of salt? Is it too little that Christ uses us in order to call the sinners to him? Are we perhaps grumbling when the last will be first and the first last? Are we not content with God's grace, which is sufficient for life, but besiege him with a catalogue of desired bonuses which he does not want to give us at this moment? Do we shun suffering, demanding that God's ways should be less rough, if we are to tread them with joy? Are we angry that the godless are so godless, the indifferent so indifferent, the pious so passive? Do we stumble over the human weakness of the pastors, the consistories, or the bishops and make an issue out of nothing, while tearing down real greatness? Are we like Israel on its way through the desert, which constantly despaired and grumbled and thus forfeited the promised land? Does fear of men prevent our ears from hearing and our mouth from proclaiming? Do we pass the time of our inner and innermost life in devising mischief, and thus bypass the chief gift, God's grace, and end up in damnation? Do we preach salvation from all sins, from death and the power of the devil, because we ourselves need this proclamation for our salvation from the coming wrath? Are our minds captured by possible oncoming catastrophes to such a degree that we no longer look for the coming Lord who will make a new heaven and a new earth?

We must let these questions stand as they are. The answers to them will determine whether the Marxist world will become the good soil on which the Word bears fruit a hundredfold. They will determine the nature of our mission which lies at our footstep. The Christian churches in North Africa and the Middle East failed at this point long before the rise of Islam. This is, therefore, the real reason for their doom, rather than the impressive power of Allah, his prophet, and his followers!

Lastly, if we submit ourselves to the proclamation of the gospel, we shall be entitled, through God's grace, to accept the Marxist rulers of the state as God's servants and agents, and to acknowledge their functions. Through them God brings about a certain measure of peace, justice, freedom, and humanity without which human life would become physically impossible. We may count on this fact, recognize it, and be grateful for it. The gospel puts things in their place, it gives us sound eyes gratefully to see justice, freedom, humanity, peace, and order as God's good gifts, provided in the Marxist realm. We must point out these positive things because we are assured by God's promise that he will not desert his creation, that he will not cause another flood to come. On this basis, we can take our place in the Marxist world, work for good wherever it has to be done, and avoid evil. Because of the gospel, this world provides room for life and is not hell. Even the Marxists are enforcing divine justice, either in accordance with or in conflict with their theoretical knowledge, because God's justice never surrenders to Marxist ideology. We are never beyond the reach of our creator and preserver, not even under the Marxists. They, too, are under his ordinance to reward the good and punish the bad. The Lord himself has set about to resist chaos, in spite of our constant attempts to foster it.

It is a fundamental truth, although it is a miracle, that we can do good in spite of being evil. If the Marxist think that they can eliminate God, or what they conceive God to be, they must be told that "he who sits in heaven laughs; the Lord has them in derision," for the Gentiles conspire and the peoples plot in vain. Christians belie their unbelief when they maintain that the degree of law and order existing in the Marxist realm is not law and order at all, because it is dominated by a materialistic world-view and motivated by historical materialism. Admittedly, Augustine said that the virtues of the Gentiles were merely glorified vices, but he denied his faith in this case. Faith discovers with amazement that even the ideological fanatic is firmly and inescapably in the grip of the heavenly Father who allows us to execute the plans of our evil hearts only in exceptional cases. Christians must stick to this truth even under very un-Christian authorities and systems. They must be free to expect good and not evil from these authorities, and to respect and help them in this high office.

Two further clarifications are necessary in order to avoid misunderstanding. It is obvious that the Marxist state departs in many important aspects from the type of government which was developed during the last centuries in Central and Western Europe as well

as in North America, and which today provides the
norm for recognizing a state as law-abiding. Even in
these territories there has always been the painful difference between ideal and reality. The concept of liberal democracy must be carefully distinguished from
its embodiment in a particular government. Nevertheless, it is an undeniable fact that there is a more
or less open field for Christians and Christian
churches in the political life of those countries, for
basing their lives on God's command and for making
known their views in public.

However, the task of Christians to recognize and
accept political responsibility in accordance with
their faith and their ethics is commensurate to the
opportunities which are actually open to them in any
given situation. From what we have said, it follows
that all Christians are under the obligation to preserve and to strengthen the basis for justice and humanity, for freedom and peaceful coexistence, and to
keep them from being transformed into arbitrari-
ness, barbarism, slavery, and the battle of all against
all, i.e., the tyranny of one group over all others. This
fundamental obligation is common to all Christians
regardless of the form of government and of the particular situation in which they find themselves. It in-
cludes the emperor who confesses Christ as well as
the prisoner who calls on the Lord. But the measure
and the means of fulfilling this obligation changes
from one situation to the other, from generation to
generation, from state to state. Under no circum-

stances can the church consider herself as being released from her political responsibility. Nor must she ever be content with the *status quo*. God sees to it that we can never sit back with folded hands regardless of how Christian a state may call itself or how many privileges it may grant to the church. On the contrary, she will be especially suspicious in such a moment of any attempt to cover up basic human malice in the name of Jesus Christ. History provides numerous illustrations of this danger.

If the church trusts in the gracious promise of Romans 13, she will set out to work courageously and confidently, knowing that she is the co-worker of him whose ordinance is effective and will remain so until the end of time. She will not overestimate the importance of differences between forms of government. She will not develop some sort of political metaphysics by absolutizing those forms which approximate most closely her faith and God's command. This is particularly important in those countries where the government is identified with a non-Christian religion, e.g., in Egypt and Persia, or with a papist ideology, e.g., in Spain and Colombia, as well as in the Marxist world. In all these places she will participate in the political life for the common good and according to the measure of possibilities open to her. She will act in the assurance that the God who uses his servants in these countries is the Father of Jesus Christ and calls them to obedience in public life. This assurance does by no means eliminate the differences between forms of governments, and most certainly not between good and evil. It would be an obdurate church which could be deaf toward the cries of the "strangers, widows, and orphans." She is under obligation to care for them and to seek justice in their behalf, even if it meant the risk of possessions, profession, career, freedom, or, in extreme cases, life itself. An obedient church will at all times be found on the side of those who suffer injustice and are shortchanged. It cannot be denied that the history of all churches is rich with examples of negligence and guilt in this respect. The church in the Marxist world would, however, heap guilt upon guilt by resigning at this point on the basis that everything was lost in her situation. Such an attitude springs from faith in a liberal ideal. But faith in Jesus Christ opens possibilities everywhere for responsible action.

Finally, it is conceivable that times and situations will arise in the Marxist world when there will be no room for Christians to participate even in the most general way in the political life according to their insights. In fact, the church has passed through times when the mere confession of Jesus Christ entailed condemnation. In Colombia and Indonesia people are dying today for the sake of Christ's name! The fear is justified that some day a similar situation could develop in the Marxist world. But even in these boundary situations the church owes the gospel of salvation to her fellow men and her rulers, and this obligation has absolute priority over any other possible or demanded course of action.

The church was founded on the witness of Jesus Christ, and she lives by this witness. If all the other possibilities are closed to her, the witness remains and, especially at that moment, it is under the promise of the Spirit who will lay words into the mouths of the witnesses. Even suffering will not shut her mouth: the praise of God takes priority over everything. The strongest objection against any kind of revolt in such moments strikes at the very heart of the gospel: How could the church make people believe in the good news of the justification of the godless while she fights them with arms? When Peter did it in Gethsemane in an exemplary fashion, he merely succeeded in cutting off Malchus' ear, which should have heard the message of the crucified. How many times did the church make the hearing impossible for her adversaries and lose herself the ability to hear the crucified, when she offered this type of resistance, sometimes with very obvious and stringent reasons! In the farewell letters to his wife before his execution in 1944, Count Moltke of Kreisau affirms once more that he was opposed to the conspiracy of the 20th of July until he was arrested, months before the attempt on Hitler's life (only thereafter the Kreisau circle decided to participate in the elimination of Hitler). These letters are a clearer and more unequivocal proclamation of the crucified than word and deed of the conspirators. The church, whether under Marxism or not, owes to it the gospel, even if every other action would thereby become impossible. But if the church *outside* the Marxist world does not recognize that the Marxists are first and last those to whom the gospel must be addressed, the witness of the church *inside* the Marxist world loses its credibility, and becomes rightly suspect, a mere tactics. The realization of this fact by the church outside would result in a change of her speaking about and against Marxism and of her actions in political affairs.